The Miracle of Sam

Sam Sitting in his Chair

The Miracle of Sam

A Story of Love and Adaptability

Michael Harris

Copyright © 2013 by Michael Harris.
Copyedited by Mark Nell Mendoza.

Library of Congress Control Number:		2013900250
ISBN:	Hardcover	978-1-4797-7546-0
	Softcover	978-1-4797-7545-3
	Ebook	978-1-4797-7547-7

This book was printed in the United States of America.

To order additional copies of this book, contact:
Xlibris Corporation
1-888-795-4274
www.Xlibris.com
Orders@Xlibris.com
116328

I would like to thank the following individuals who either helped with this manuscript or were influential in some manner to its origination.

Rebecca Bramon, who provided wonderful hand-painted images which you will see following some of the chapters, including the one above.

Patricia Kayne, Molly, and Wes, who have been Sam's most constant walking companions since his arrival with Linda and me.

Cyndie and Mike Koopsen, who showed Sam and me the beautiful Sedona area on foot, one trail at a time, accompanied by Sam's girlfriend Ellie.

And most importantly, Linda Kay, my wife and Sam's favorite female human, who added her hard work and personality to this manuscript.

*Sam can be reached at this e-mail address shown on his web page:

themiracleofsam.com

This book is dedicated to
Sam
who saved my life.
And to
Linda Kay
who makes life worth living.

TABLE OF CONTENTS

THE MIRACLE OF SAM

Everyone has a story. This is Sam's.

According to Doc, the best vet in Sedona (and perhaps the civilized world), Sam began his life as an unexpected arrival at one of the recently targeted puppy mills just outside of town. His mom, a blond golden retriever, took an unscheduled walk in the neighborhood and came back with child. Wiley Coyote was the father.

Six of the seven puppies had Mom's beautiful characteristics and appearance, which meant $400 or more per head in revenue for the puppy mill. Sam, however, had short alert ears, a smaller build, and pretty much mirrored Dad's features; so instead of a good home with some rich Sedona family, he was headed for the local humane society.

Sam spent the next eighteen months in and out of various homes; each one of them tied him to a tree in the front or backyard and left him there all day, alone and without any level of attention, love, or affection. Being the resourceful pup he was, he quickly escaped each one of these forms of confinement, winding up back at the pound for the fourth time in January of the year 2009. The last time he came back to the kennels, he still had a piece of the rope, which he had chewed through, around his neck.

That's where I come in . . .

Linda and I had a terrible 2008, with huge financial damage, a bad year which culminated in the loss of our precious golden retriever Sarah to valley fever near the end of December. Linda felt it might be a good idea to peruse the local humane society to find a new friend, though I was pretty much out of it and not too enthusiastic.

I was at a personal low when I first met Sam. He looked sadly over the small gate at the humane society kennel and stood on his back feet, leaning against the gate as we reviewed the various options available. He never barked or whined and was conspicuously silent above the loud barking and high noise level. He was in for his fourth visit to the kennel since his birth and obviously didn't care for the noise and high level of activity going on around him. I think we both were ready for a change to the good. It goes without saying that we kind of took to each other, and he came home with us.

God works strangely and magnificently in our lives. I've seen his work many times, and though I have significant technical and physical science education, I still can see his handprints in everything around me. There is a tremendous spiritual balance in everything we touch and see on a daily basis that normally goes unrecognized. Chance meetings which change our lives forever for the better are some of the best things he gives us.

My Higher Power was definitely there early in 2009 when I needed him most, and through him, I met Sam. This wonderful gift from God, at eighteen months old, took me out of my severe depression and gave me a new and positive outlook on life. I owe him my life many times over, and that's why I'm writing his story, even though many chapters are yet to be experienced or written.

Please enjoy this small look into how the kindness and love from a small, wonderful creature of God saved me and my family.

Sam on Couch

 CHAPTER 1

Sam knew he didn't belong here. Everyone is noisy and very confident that their every need will be provided. This level of complacency is not in his nature. He doesn't feel like he fits here. Mom doesn't really look like him, except for her color, and her floppy ears mirror the other brothers and sisters that came along with him on this cold winter morning.

The first thing he remembers is that all of them are gathered up and weighed, then allowed to feed, with Mom generously providing nourishment in the customary way. She seems to love him as much as the others. At least that makes him a bit more comfortable for the time being.

During his stay here, all of the caretakers constantly handled him and looked him over. There was wonder in their eyes about just what made him different from the rest; he could feel it and see it in their puzzled expressions. There was also fear, when they looked into his eyes and saw what was inside. They knew he had a side to him that didn't fit their objectives, and he knew the first time he was held that he would not remain in their lives.

He was the first to walk, the first to take dry nourishment, and the first to jump the wire enclosure and go on a three-day walk outside. He was also the first to find out what happens when you are bad. He often tried to play with his siblings, but they were much too round and slow to be of much interest to him. He really liked the rabbits and squirrels, as they were much more active and challenged him often.

"You really dropped the ball this time," Vince muttered to Val as he met her eyes with a stare of disdain. Val, it turns out, was in control of the facility during the night her female golden charge was visited by an outside entity, which was later determined to be a coyote male.

They were both looking at a beautiful pride of golden babies, perfect in every way, except for the smaller one with very peculiar appearance and behavior.

"He's only the one. The rest are perfect, and we don't have to let anyone know about what we've seen here tonight. I'll get rid of that one as soon as the Humane Society will take him." Valerie spoke with the knowledge and experience of a veteran puppy mill employee.

As they reviewed the new brood, they were looking at over two thousand dollars in revenue, already spending it in their simple minds. Val had an "in" at the local Humane Society, so bringing in a young puppy without explanation would be an easy task, and one already forgotten. The "Vs" were well known and respected in the community, particularly since their little puppy farm was well concealed and unknown to any of the local residents. Their other persona reflected their artistic tendencies, and that is for which they were well known.

One day, while Sam was wandering around outside the fenced area, he came across a scent he seemed to know—that of a strange animal just beyond his hearing and vision. The smell seemed very familiar to him, yet nothing he could identify. He heard a calling, first from this creature and then from the nearby hills, one which made him both cautious and strangely comfortable at the same time. He would hear this calling often while staying at this place.

This behavior went on for a couple of moons, and then one day, he was separated from the rest. He was taken to an enclosed building with many other small and large dogs (the Humane Society, for us humans), and during the next few moons, he called this home. The caretakers here were very nice, and also very curious about just who he was.

Once he acclimated to the Humane Society, Sam began to think of these humans as caregivers instead of caretakers. They wanted nothing from him, yet gave him everything he needed. Thus, it became obvious to Sam that there was at least one significant distinction between humans. This knowledge made him much more capable of making decisions related to humans as time passed. He decided at once that he would only accept the companionship of caregivers going forward.

Marc was the first to see Sam when he was brought in by Val. It would be many months before Sam was to have this name given to him. He would have several other names in the interim; however, none of them really belonged to him. *Sam* was to be the only real name for him.

"And who is this young fellow?" he asked Valerie?

"We found him wandering around the foundry a week ago and fattened him up a bit," Valerie lied. "He's pretty cute for a little bugger, but as you know, we already have a couple pups of our own, so here he is."

"He won't be hard to place. He's a cute little fellow," Mark said as Valerie handed him over.

Marc looked at the wild face, obviously full of intellect from an unknown derivation. The little fellow looked Marc directly in the eye, something he had never experienced from any dog before. He imagined several pedigree options, but none fit Sam's profile, so he gave up and listed him as a "golden mix" on the card that would later be found on the entrance to Sam's new digs.

During his stay at this place, Sam was given a calling ("Buddah," for the beach on which he spent most of his escape time) and was described to other humans as a "golden mix" with an activity level of "rock and roll."

Life here was uneventful, until he was allowed to walk among the dogs. He was feared by most, even though he was very small. They knew there was something different about him. Several of them tried to attack and hurt him, but they soon found out this was not a good idea for them. Sam was much stronger and very much faster and knew what they were thinking before they did, and he was quick to correct their actions when necessary to defend himself.

Though he was comfortable here, he knew this was not going to work for him in the long term. Sam was not to be kept in an enclosed area for very long. He saw several opportunities to leave, but each time he tried, he was caught in the act, so he became known as the "escape artist" by the caregivers.

Sam knew from experience that canines were destined to come and go from this place with the high walls. He'd seen it many times before. Humans came and went and often left with a new companion, so he knew one day he would be out of here.

Something in him longed to be back in the open, like he was when he escaped from his place of birth so many moons ago. He knew the open was where his father could be found. He sensed and felt his father's presence just beyond the enclosed fence at his place of birth many times while living with his mom and siblings.

The First Adoption

One fine sunny day in June, a mature couple came in and visited Sam. Sam was about six months old and cute as a little bunny. Because of his strong build, he looked much older to the casual observer. They fell in love with him and decided to take him home, and once there, they tied him to a tree in their large backyard. He had a job now, and that job was to keep people and other things out of the yard. He was never allowed inside, even in the rain, and became accustomed to being left for days without food or water.

Dan Mondale was tall and lean and smelled of cannabis and rye grass which, when combined, provided Dan and Laura a discreet method of sustenance. They needed an active and alert companion who would notify them when someone came to visit unannounced, and Sam fit the bill. They named him "Skipper" and gave him a place beneath a large tree where he could see the entire yard, including the cash crop surrounding him and his tree.

"This fellow looks like a good fit. What do you think?" Dan asked of Laura. She was listening to the incessant barking from a young shepherd mix in the cage next door to Sam and replied, "Cute, but maybe a bit too nice, don't you think?"

"He seems to be very alert to things going on around him, and I think he'll let us know if anyone comes by. Let's give him a try and see what happens. I think the shepherd might draw too much attention," Dan cautiously replied.

Laura—the one wearing the pants in the family—agreed, making the decision to take Sam/Skipper. She asked Marc to draw up the paperwork, and off they went, over to the big tree amidst the illegal harvest.

Being the strong silent type, Sam never barked or complained, so he was the ideal candidate for this job according to the caretakers who took him from the shelter. The only problem for Sam was the confinement. He could deal with water and food deprivation, as it was well within his biological structure to handle these issues, and weather had absolutely no effect on him. He wanted to be free, however.

After one moon had passed, Sam and the pot crop received a

visitor. The strange scent that Sam experienced at the puppy mill was back, and Sam came face to face with someone who looked a lot like him but was slightly larger in build and presence. This creature walked slowly over to him, gave him a good looking-over, helped himself to the remaining food in the dish alongside Sam, and cautiously exited.

Sam felt a strange attachment to this unusually strong and silent creature and also experienced some of the feelings he had while lying alongside his mother. As the creature left, Sam—who was half coyote and half dog—also felt the same feelings he had when he was separated from his mom, and just like that time, neither said or did anything. Sam was beginning to understand his roots.

The next evening, he chewed through the rope around his neck and left for the nearby creek and woods. He didn't know what he would find there, but he thought of his father and the options that might present themselves in the days and weeks ahead. Anything would be better than confinement, and Sam looked forward to this new opportunity.

Free at Last

Sam the coyote found his calling. He made a den near the running creek, from which he could hunt, and hunting was very good. He learned to catch squirrels by climbing up the trees a branch at a time, until the squirrel had to try and get past him to escape. He also found out that rabbits had the habit of running in large circles, with the intent of being back where they began once a chase was over. He evolved a method of getting them to run, and then he would meet them head-on as they circled back.

On days when hunting was scarce, Sam the dog found that KFC made a great alternative, and humans seldom ate everything they procured. The local storage place for uneaten food (*trash bin* for you humans reading this) was a weekly destination for Sam. He learned quickly how to separate meat from bone, as this type of food had dangerous and sharp bones. Other food provided bones which were less sharp and quite flavorful, but these bones were very lethal and were to be avoided.

On his third day free, Sam was visited by the Others. They were similar to the one that visited Sam while he was with the caretakers in their backyard, but this group had no love for Sam whatsoever. The big one wanted to hurt him, but the other five just backed away, partially from fear and partially because the big one wished it. Sam knew at that moment what it was like to be considered a food group.

As the big one approached, Sam withdrew into his den, which was fortunately made from solid rock in a shape that accommodated Sam and little else. This fact saved Sam for the time being; however, Sam knew he would have to be cautious from now on, as the Others were likely to revisit him on occasion. Tonight, Sam would sleep, though very cautiously, as each little noise caused him to awaken.

Over the next few weeks, Sam became very proficient at managing his environment. He improved his den to accommodate the few things he liked to collect: bones, a plastic bottle that crunched when he played with it, a squeaky thing left behind by a visiting puppy, and the tail of a jackrabbit. These things provided nocturnal enjoyment on those evenings in which he found sleep too evasive.

Evenings brought other problems as well. Many times, drunken humans would come to the creek and throw bottles onto the rocks, breaking them into a myriad of pieces, which was making walking difficult, and evasive measures were nearly impossible when confronted by the Others.

Several times a week, the Others came to visit with malice on their minds. Each time, the smaller ones held back, and the big one tried to coax him out of his comfortable den. After much scratching and snarling, the big one moved off to try easier prey. Though Sam found this process frustrating, he found this lifestyle infinitely superior to living on the end of a rope in someone's backyard.

He's Back . . .

After several months on his own, Sam was having trouble keeping food down, and he had other digestive issues as well, making him a bit slower and less in control. Something he ate or drank was making life miserable for him, so he decided to make himself visible to the human world. As he knew would happen, a young caregiver took him in and dropped him off at the same humane society building where he was first taken while very young. This turned out to be the best thing that could happen. After a few days of medicine and nourishment, he was well again and back on his feet.

It was just like he had never left, except there were several new faces, all of whom welcomed him back.

Marc looked over Sam as he was led back into the center. "Look who's back," he said. "I guess the odd couple lost you, and it's a good thing. They were up to no good, anyway."

Sam didn't understand any of these words, but he sensed the meaning. He was pretty good at judging and reasoning the words of humans. He was led to a nearby gate, which Marc opened for him.

He had a roommate who was a smaller, older, but a very nice shepherd mix. For the next five weeks, he and the shepherd enjoyed each other's company, learning from each other as dogs and coyotes often do. The shepherd learned how to project fear into the larger dogs that used to pick on him, keeping them at bay for the first time in his young life. He, in return, taught Sam how to play—something Sam had never experienced. They tossed and turned much of the evening while the other dogs whined and barked and slept most of the day, when the caregivers kept the other dogs quiet.

Sam never got used to the strange dry food he was given, even though the shepherd showed him how to eat. He never put on weight like the other dogs, so everyone was concerned about his health, and the caregivers spent a lot of time trying to induce him to eat more. He just didn't have the need to eat the quantity of food the caregivers felt was appropriate for him, primarily because it wasn't in his makeup. They would learn why later.

While in the exercise yard with the other dogs, Sam seemed a bit aloof. He spent much of the time watching each of the other dogs' behavior and kept notes. The big ones liked to bully the smaller ones, and the smaller ones became quite adept at evasion and avoidance. The big ones learned quickly not to mess with Sam, after he had a discussion with the first one who attempted to hurt him.

Through careful observation such as this, Sam learned quickly about the pecking order among canines. It all started the first day Sam was back. A huge black dog decided to have Sam for lunch, and it ran at him with mouth open and mind shut. Sam sidestepped him, grabbed him by the neck, and threw him against the wall.

Before the huge dog could rise, Sam put his mouth around his neck and held him to the ground, talking to him through his slightly closed mouth. After Sam rose, the big dog continued to lie on the ground and wouldn't make eye contact with Sam for more than an hour. Just like prison guards, the caregivers missed this act completely. Sam liked the pecking order. It brought him a huge amount of respect and allowed him to do pretty much as he pleased without any other canine pestering him.

After this, Sam had no issues from any of the other large dogs. Apparently, bad news travels fast in the big-dog world. To this day, when Sam goes back to visit the humane society building, the big dogs all go to a neutral corner, and the smaller dogs welcome him with open arms.

Sam was becoming larger himself. He now weighed in at nearly fifty pounds—about twice as much as he weighed when first adopted. He was a very handsome pup, with flowing golden hair, wild eyes, and a wolflike appearance. His legs were longer than a golden retriever's, his head and feet were larger than a coyote's, and his tail, large and fluffy like a golden's, was well articulated like a coyote's.

Needless to say, his strange compelling beauty got him adopted a second time within the year. This time, a single male caregiver took him home to a ranch in the nearby area, with a very large backyard and something very strange growing in a huge greenhouse out back.

Once again, Sam experienced one of the weaknesses of the human kind. He was picked to guard an illegal crop, but this time, the crop was intended for personal use only.

Victor Reyes knew a good guard when he saw one. Of the dozens of dogs in the shelter, Sam was the most alert, in the best condition, and he seemed to be an ideal choice for this particular task.

Marc had a few trepidations about letting Sam go this time. He was uncomfortable with the proposed adoptive parent, and not just because he was single. Victor seemed to have a need rather than a desire to adopt, and this concerned Marc. Unfortunately, Marc had to follow procedure.

"He's the one," Victor stated briefly. "Let's get the paperwork going. I have to get back in an hour or so."

Victor was over six feet tall and very handsome, but unattached.

He had jet-black hair swept back, with a short ponytail which he tucked in and under his cap. The ladies loved him, but in his occupation of choice, permanent companionship was risky. If anyone discovered his little backyard nursery, his job with the Fire Department would be in jeopardy.

"Follow me," was all Marc said, as he smoldered inside quietly. He also quietly hoped Sam would and could escape this adoption, as he had so skillfully exited his prior unacceptable situation. He yearned to see Sam again, and soon.

Sam was in and out rather quickly this time. The pothead just needed a guard for his greenhouse, and Sam was in no mood to be tied up yet again. He chewed through the rope, and when he found his way back to the shelter with a rope still tied around his neck, the pothead thought it better to allow him to remain there.

Marc was there when Sam returned and gave him a big hug. Sam cuddled with Marc for a few minutes while his fenced area was prepared, and he entered without any urging. He was very tired and very happy to be back.

After he was settled in, Marc stopped by to visit. Sam had just covered ten miles to get back to the shelter this time and was pretty worn out when he finally got there; and of course, he was welcomed back with loving arms, food, and a now too-familiar roof over his head.

"We'll do a better job next time, I promise," Marc said to Sam as Sam lay down to rest, seemingly ignorant of the constant barking and noise around him.

And So, Once Again . . .

The older couple was sad; he could feel it. Sam knew he could make a difference in their lives if he moved in with them, so he willingly went with the caregiver pair when they selected him from the three candidates. Sam didn't know for sure where he would be, or if he would like it, but again he was getting tired of being confined and longed to be outside these walls, so off he went.

Marc looked at the couple. They had recently lost their mature yellow Lab to an extended illness and were ready to be happy again. Sam seemed to be a good choice for them, and likewise.

Karen and George Slater lived in a gated community with walls surrounding each parcel of land, making unsolicited visits nearly impossible. They were carefully polled by Marc.

"Will he have the home to himself, or do you have any other pets?" Marc cautiously inquired.

"He'll love it there," Karen offered. "We have lots of room and a nice wall around the yard. He'll have lots of room to romp without being bothered."

"He is so cute and loving. We miss our Sally, but he'll more than make up for our loss. Thank you for making this so easy," George added.

A ten-minute drive later, Sam was introduced to his new home. Once again, he found himself living outside, which was fine with him. This time, a six-foot wall separated him from forest land, and though the food was better and provided daily, he still felt limited by the confines of the huge wall.

The couple must have experienced a common loss because their sadness was very strong and not easily swayed. Sam played with them on the rare occasion that they ventured outside their lair into the yard, and during that time, both of them seemed to forget their sadness, and this made Sam feel needed.

After two moons, the couple went away for a week, and during that time, Sam was cared for by a younger couple who were less accommodating with food and water. It was during that time Sam decided he needed to explore the other side of the wall, and a quick jump later, he was outside and free again.

After following his nose to the KFC, he was reoriented with his original territory, and after grabbing a back and a leg, made off toward his den. Satisfied from his meal, he slept the remainder of the evening without incident.

As Sam fell back into his routine, so did the things around him. One of those things was the Others. During his absence, Sam had put on about twenty-nine pounds and doubled in length. He was no longer the pup the Others had mistreated, and they were about to find this out.

The big one came over to the den, and Sam stepped outside. He dropped his head below his shoulders and made direct eye contact with the big one. There was a moment of doubt in the big one's eyes, and that was all the advantage Sam needed to attack. Sam immediately ran toward him, covering the fifty feet in a fraction of the blink of an eye.

Before the big one could perceive what had happened, he was lying on his back with Sam standing over him, a mouth full of teeth showing. On this bright and sunny day, the rules changed forever. The pack dispersed while Sam had a discussion with the big one, and after that day, the Others became the hunted. Sam was afraid no more, and for the first time in a long while, he slept and dreamed as never allowed before. He still kept track of each and every little noise, however.

Guess Who's Back

Sam was more than a year old when he got sick again, and like before, he knew how to get better. His newly acquired girlfriend Mia, a collie-shepherd mix, asked to go with him, and he allowed her to accompany him. He wandered over to a meeting place for the caregivers and, once again, allowed himself to be taken to the shelter. He knew the routine, and again after a couple of weeks, was much better. It must be something in the water making him sick, he thought. Surely, the KFC wasn't the issue.

Back at the shelter, Marc put Sam and Mia in the same room, and life was good. Sam then introduced Mia to some of the other fellows who were still in residence, and all got along famously. Though he came in sick, he was still not bothered by any of the other dogs, as his reputation preceded him. The caregivers were becoming accustomed to him and often took him out for walks both alone and with Mia.

"You're a real trooper. I hope someone perfect gets you next time," Marc told Sam during his trek around the pretty grounds which surrounded the shelter. Sam looked back at Marc with affection and understanding. He knew Marc had his best interest in mind and was both pleased and comforted by this understanding. When they returned to the shelter, Sam was feeling much better.

He still didn't care for the food, but Mia really enjoyed it, so he allowed her to eat nearly all of the dry stuff. He learned to climb trees much better the last time out, so the squirrels that resided in his walking area provided him with sustenance, despite his caregiver's attempts to keep him from obtaining this delicacy.

Sam learned while eating KFC to avoid the small bones, which could cause him harm if consumed, and noted that the KFC caregivers seemed to hate picking up after he left them behind. It was the same here. Sam could hear the shelter caregivers complaining about which one of them had pickup detail, though none of them punished him for this, or anything else for that matter.

One day in January, shortly after his eighteenth month alive, he heard a couple of humans come through the door. There was something different about them. He could feel a mutual and tremendous sense of loss for one of his kind, and though the pair looked at every one of the first group of dogs and talked to and touched many of them, they didn't see what they hoped to find.

Sam was outside with the second group of dogs, and he watched them through the semi-transparent doggie door.

He was so transfixed by them that he nearly forgot to come in and say hi. Mia was entertaining them as he stepped inside, and Sam felt a strange bond with them as he gently pushed Mia aside and stood his full length against the fence, so he could be touched by the couple. He laid his ears flat against his head (something reserved for the most intimate situations) and let them scratch him behind the ears.

Marc and Linda were already talking about Sam, calling him Buddah, as his name plate showed.

"Is he a golden mix? He looks a little small for one, except for his head and feet." There was a pause, and then "I think Mike kind of likes him," Linda said in brief. "One thing for sure—that name's got to go."

Marc thought to himself. "This might be a good fit. They both seem nice and stable, and Sam (Buddah) is thinking the same thing."

"Those two seem to get along pretty well. How about a test drive to see if everyone gets along?" Marc offered.

"I think that's a great idea. What is the next step?" Linda asked of Marc.

"Just follow me, and we'll do some paperwork." Marc was pretty excited about this placement, and in his heart, he knew everyone was going to benefit.

Linda was watching Mike and Sam. Mike was already calling him Sam, so from today forward, he would be Sam, the coydog. Sam was already responding to his new name, and within a few days, he had forgotten the old ones.

Sam looked up at Mike, his new caregiver, and Linda, Mike's mate. He knew he was going home with them when the male caregiver's face changed color and his eyes became moist. Though they left him there that day, he knew they would be back; and three days later, they came back. When they left, he went with them. Something in Sam told him this was one of the best days in his life, and that his life just changed for the better. Sam was pretty intuitive by now. He had been with several humans over the last year and a half, and each had peculiarities which distinguished them from other humans.

This couple was unique in that they had a tremendous amount of love for Sam. He knew his new life was going to be much different than he had experienced to date, and his heart was filled with optimism and excitement. He eagerly looked forward to the days ahead.

Sam Walking Kel Fox Trail

CHAPTER 2

Sam didn't know anything about this, but the things talked about below would shape his life from the moment Sam and I first met. These events, taken singly, would not have made any difference in the average life; but when shoved together, they bore down on Mike and Linda like a lead balloon. To start things off, a company which made a practice of stealing from its employees closed its doors without warning, and the crooks who ran it fled the country. This started things out late in 2007, and things got worse from there. The only thing Sam knew for sure was that he was both needed and wanted: something he had never felt before.

Mike's story

I found myself without work and ethically responsible for the welfare of a dozen employees living from paycheck to paycheck. The events which occurred on this sunny day in September were first noticed as the early employee came to the front door and found it chained shut. After repeated attempts to contact the company president, and then the other officers one at a time, the employee and the remaining personnel who came to work that day got a hold of me in Arizona.

"Mike, what's going on?" These were the first words I heard that morning. The stock manager had a strong sense of urgency in his voice. "The doors are locked and chained shut, and I don't see anything left on the assembly floor through the front window."

I spent most of that day, and every day during the rest of September, trying to make sense of the situation. I drove to San Diego and had a special friend of mine look into things. In a couple of days, we pieced together the story.

The several months before September apparently had not been kind to the investors, so they decided to walk out on this lucrative but fairly small venture and skip town, each escaping to their respective offshore homes. They had a "yard sale" the evening before, long after hours, and liquidated all the equipment and furniture, leaving only partially assembled customers' work in progress remaining and a moderate inventory of components specific to the projects at hand.

Since I was on the business development side of the operation, I quickly liberated the parts and inventory and sent them to a group of facilities that could complete the contracts—with our help, of course. Fortunately, this move gave most of our guys something to do while they got their affairs in order, and we were able to save the projects. And some of the contractors stepped up for the San Diego personnel, came forward, and hired nearly all of the displaced workers.

It took me the better part of three months to get their lives back in order, and once I did so, I started on the remaining customers whose jobs were not completed. I spent a bit more time in San Diego than I would have liked, but I finalized the open projects and was able to firm up the engineering and technical staff and help them reenter the workplace. Finally, by the first quarter of 2008, I was able to begin focusing on my cash flow issues. I'm still working on that one.

In addition, Sarah, our golden, was going through a myriad of medical issues—none of which could be tied down to any diagnosable cause. She would get rashes; they'd disappear. She'd start limping for no apparent reason, and she had coughing spells. This went on for about a year. She would get better so quick we thought, as the doctors did, that she was having allergies, as goldens often had in this area.

To wrap things up, my wife Linda was left without health insurance, since the aforementioned company wasn't paying the premiums. The gap gave the insurance company an excuse to drop her, since she was a cancer survivor. The incumbent idiot of a president gave the insurance companies a method and capability to screen and exclude any and all insurance candidates who might be other than flawless in the health and prior condition situation, and these carriers, of course, took the opportunity to screen and exclude anyone who might ever consider placing a claim of any type.

Thus, the disastrous economic conditions virtually decimated the US middle class, and those not destroyed in this process were eliminated with extremely poor handling of the economic situation and housing disaster. This was quite a legacy, even more so than the Andrew Johnson dynasty, making 2008–2012 one of the worse economic disaster events in recorded history, in my opinion.

Well, I feel better now, having gotten that out of my system. Now let's get back to the story at hand. After all, this is Sam's story, not mine.

Everything must happen for a reason. I was primed for a significant change in my life by the time 2009 rolled around. The first thing that happened was losing our golden retriever Sarah to valley fever two days after my birthday in January.

This was not what I had in mind for a life-changing moment. I was completely caught off guard, as was my wife Linda and our doggie doctors. Sarah started having seizures, and tests found that she had a fungus in her brain that could only have been caused by valley fever. The symptoms were easily misdiagnosed as allergies or pulled muscles from hiking so that we and the doctors completely overlooked the true common cause.

Linda and I were completely devastated, and the only thing we could do was to have her put down. She was losing ground daily and long past her quality of life threshold. I took her for one last walk, and I had to carry her back, as she lost what little control she had left. After the doctor did what was needed, I took her to her favorite hiking place and buried her where she spent the best times of her life. She is still there today; both Sam and I have heard her on occasion, as have several of our mutual friends and family.

A few weeks after we lost Sarah, Linda decided we needed to visit the local humane society, so I reluctantly agreed. We walked through the new building, not really expecting to see anyone we would want to bring home. We'd been here many times before with the gift of blankets, food, and nice toys for the pups who called this place home, so several people knew us and greeted us as we arrived.

We talked for a while with them, asked some questions about new arrivals, and made conversation as people often do; however, I wasn't really there. I was several miles away, with Sarah, and was not ready to turn loose of the good memories or feelings associated with our long-term relationship.

It was Marc who met us at the elevator.

"Hey, guys, I heard about Sarah. I'm really sorry for your loss. She was a great pup," Marc offered as he met us.

Marc is tall and lean, and every eligible female in town knows where to find him. He is often found leading a moderate procession of lovelies throughout the facility, showing them the latest arrivals and discussing each as if he had raised them personally. Many have been adopted into very loving families as a result of this approach.

Today, Marc was alone, and he gave us his full attention. He had something in mind.

"It's been awhile since you two dropped by. We have some new kids I'd like you to see, if you have time."

"We have nothing but time," I muttered as Linda looked at me with concern. She knew what I was going through.

As always, Marc saved the best for last. We walked by several talkative pups—some old and some very young, some big and some very small, some loud and some quiet. They all needed a home where they could be loved like Sarah was, and one day, each of them would find exactly that kind of place.

It was nice to see the new wing and experience a humane society that would never consider putting any of its occupants down. The no-kill facilities had a completely different outlook about their residents. None of them were anything but full-time residents until they found happy owners, so each was treated with the best possible care and compassion.

This in itself made everyone involved very happy and secure, particularly the canine residents. Life without desperation is significantly more prosperous and comfortable, and all the canine residents exuded this feeling, making everyone who touched them more comfortable in their decisions. All the residents and their handlers were especially nice and well cared for. All of them that is, except for one poor individual who lived in the second row of the second building. He didn't belong here, and both of us knew it the moment we first met.

Sam and I Meet

As I rounded the second row, I saw him for the first time. Something struck me about him. I came to this place to satisfy my wife's need to snap me out of my depression by bringing something new into our lives, and since kids were out of the question, as were cats, she decided a visit here might do the trick. I would play the game to satisfy her need to help, but I had no intention of bringing anything home. I wasn't done being sad yet.

Losing Sarah left a big hole in my life. Thinking about it now, even while surrounded by so many desperate canines looking for purpose in their lives, I couldn't put myself into the spirit of giving. I was still feeling sorry for myself, and I didn't have the emotional resources to become a caregiver. I was walking through one big reminder of the sadness and loss I still carried within me and growing increasingly sad and uncomfortable.

Yet the instant I first saw Sam, something did happen. Though I was balancing my sadness on my shoulders, and doing it rather well, he kept coming to the forefront of my thoughts. All of this was happening in fractions of a second, but time seemed to stop and let me have brief control so I could gather my thoughts into at least one recognizable actionable item.

"And who's this pretty girl?" I heard Linda ask of Marc. They were still in the first row of kennels. I had strolled over to the second row by that time.

I couldn't hear Marc's reply. He has a soft voice, and Linda can be heard several counties away. They were discussing a small foot injury on the rather large female dog Linda was mooning over.

I was in my own world during that time, however. Nothing happening on that side of the fence was of any interest to me.

When Sam looked up at me from behind the one called Mia, I knew I was hooked. He looked as sad as I felt, and I knew this place wasn't for him, even though every aspect of confined life catered to his well-being and comfort. He was simply not to be confined. It was slowly destroying him. It was like I crawled inside his mind and could feel his pain and unhappiness.

I spend as much of my time as possible in non-enclosed areas, so I quickly understood what he was telling me. In my way, I let him know that if he came with us, he would never be closed in or confined and could have the life he wanted without restriction—at least, as much as we could provide. I think he heard me because he gently pushed Mia aside and reached through the cage to touch me with his head and hands.

I think I must have given him my life story in a few microseconds, and he must have approved the selection, for on that day, we became part of a pack. This was the most honorable position imaginable for a pair of misfits like us, and without either of us speaking a single word, we conveyed the greatest honor to each other.

It goes without saying that this meeting would change both our lives forever. And again, needless to say, these changes would be for the better for everyone concerned.

Marc is a mind reader. He practices it daily, and due to his many brushes with the opposite sex, he has become very good at reading people. He has been wondering for a while how best to place Sam. He wasn't going to let just anyone have him. Sam has been too many places before that didn't quite agree with his unique talents and capabilities.

Marc took a peek around the corner at me and Sam and knew immediately his job for today was done. Linda was still fooling around with the large pup around the corner, so Marc walked over to her and brought her back to me and my newfound friend.

Linda spoke first, muffled by the tears of joy she was holding inside. "That's really something." She sighed as the words came out. "I haven't seen anything quite like that. He's been down so long, I forgot what it was like to see him happy."

Marc was already grinning out loud. "Finally!" was all he said.

He shared with Linda the several escapades involving Sam and the other previous adoptees, and how Sam kept coming back. "We were just about to rename him Colonel Sanders, because he always smells of KFC when he comes back!" Marc quipped.

Linda was already joining me as Marc finished his sentence. Marc gave us a few minutes alone with Sam and slipped off to do the paperwork.

The next few weeks made a world of difference in my life. I now had a reason to live, and Sam brought out the feelings I had put away since the loss of Sarah. I could actually see the future again, and that is very significant. I lost that option when Sarah died, and I couldn't see beyond the day I was buried within.

Sam brought out the capability of planning and living beyond the day—something I was certain was gone forever. Today, I look back at this meeting and realize if this hadn't happened when it did, I might not be here today.

Linda on Sam

For Sam, it wasn't about building a taller fence, but building a home he didn't want to leave.

We had just lost our five-year-old golden Sarah to valley fever, and though devastated by our loss, our need to continue to give love to a furry companion took hold.

We made our first visit to the new Humane Society of Sedona. Once there, we strolled past forlorn faces and wagging tails. It was my husband Mike who spotted Sam in one of the last stalls. I was taken by a much-too-big "Sadie" to notice the bonding going on. By the time we got home to "discuss" the possibility of bringing Mike's find home, we had already named him and were making plans for his homecoming.

On his first night home, he used the doggie door and slept on the bed with us all night. I figured he was a keeper. The rest could be taught.

Sam had been a stray and wound up at the shelter at least three times in his eighteen months of life. The last time, he arrived with a rope around his neck that had been chewed through. When we brought him home, he was very skittish and tried tirelessly to jump the fence. Our plan to make him want to stay began.

With daily trips in the jeep to the forest to run and chase rabbits and chipmunks, lots of good food, and cuddles, he began to settle down. He didn't know how to eat food from a dish. He would take a mouthful and put it on the floor and then eat. He also seemed to prefer drinking out of a water bottle. He didn't know what a toy was, and the game of fetch left him with a puzzled look on his face. Sadly, he had never been truly loved.

When we found him, he had ribs sticking out, and his backbone was very visible. No more. He is a healthy, happy, and very loving family member.

He has traveled to New Mexico and San Diego. It was in San Diego, where we take him for walks on the beach, that he taught himself how to body surf. Mike had thrown a piece of seaweed into the surf, and Sam went in after it. He was suddenly lifted up and delivered to shore by a small wave. The rest is history. He loved it. Into the water he went, again and again. I could swear I saw a smile on his face.

Since Sam is part coyote, he brings leftover pieces of rabbit and deer to us on our hikes here in Sedona. His job, it seems, is to provide for his pack. He loves to go to the school on weekends and play with his many dog friends, greeting them one and all with kisses.

Sam doesn't bark, but howls when he wants to go for a hike. The golden in him loves to lean and cuddle. What a great companion he has come to be. We love him with all our hearts. He was a little late for Christmas, but just in time for us.

Sam's Profile at Turkey Creek

CHAPTER 3

Sam looked upon his new caregiver and knew he would not and should not mess up this living arrangement. He had a unique opportunity to build a different type of relationship—one which would last a lifetime, and one which would yield happiness and comfort the likes of which he had never experienced.

How he knew this was beyond his ken, but he knew. It was very much like how he felt and understood the first time he saw his dad after being away so long. The instant he first saw him, he knew this strong and beautiful creature was his kin. He was now a pack member, and that feeling brought him closer to knowing who he was.

After being with the first batch of caregivers, Sam knew something better was in store for him, and that unlike the other humans he'd encountered to date, someone special was out there somewhere. Now, his current situation reaffirmed his beliefs.

He knew he was in a safe place and never wanted to leave this place, so he was very careful, and for once, he sincerely behaved as he knew he should around caregivers. He knew he was both loved and respected. In turn, he gave the new caregiver what he needed: a kind and caring companion who knew his pain, one who knew how to help make it go away.

The First Hike Near My Old Home

As I jumped into the car again, I was very concerned. Was I going back to the shelter place? Was I rejected so early once again? No, this isn't the way. I know all too well the way back to the place. This is different.

I know where we are. We are on the opposite side of the running water, and suddenly, a peace comes over me like no feeling I have ever experienced. My caregiver walks with me, and I stay near, though surrounding us is a large quantity of things I would like to chase and catch. I sense that there will be time for that later, and I patiently behave as I believe the caregiver would like me to act.

This goes on for a short time, and then I switch personalities. My tail drops down like my father's, no longer perched in a semicircle across my back, and I began to lope like my father, searching for something to capture for dinner.

My caregiver is nearby and says nothing as I crisscross the trail ahead of us. Several times, my caregiver stealthily hides or changes direction, but I always know exactly where he is hiding, and I always return to him once my exploration of this scent or that one is over.

He seems surprised that I can always find him, and he often tries to scare me, only to realize that just before he makes his move, I detect his intentions and turn around to look directly at him. He shows a combination of frustration and amazement at my abilities.

Together, we move through familiar areas and into new territory for me. We walk for a quarter daylight time and go to some places I have heard of but have never explored. My father told me of this place on a visit, leaking the information of a large number of rabbits in the area and my favorite chasing thing: javelina. I find his report to be true as we walk into an area without caregiver scent, and two large rabbits with very long ears offer the opportunity of pursuit.

My caregiver has placed a noisy thing on my collar, and it makes beeping sounds that distract my hearing, but I can still hear the rapid heartbeats of both rabbits. This type of rabbit is very fast and can jump nearly as high as me; but though it is very fast, I am faster.

I catch up to the first rabbit as it dives into a large spiny bush, and I know from experience to jump over this bush. The rabbit is smart enough to take a few spiny spears on the chin in order to save its life. I return to the caregiver, satisfied that I have done my best.

The caregiver removes the noisy thing and looks in obvious amazement at it, back to me, and then back to it. He pushes on it, and the noise stops, and he looks at me, very pleased. He says the words "forty-five point two mph"—which, of course, means nothing to me. We walk some more, and though nothing of interest shows itself, we both enjoy the experience.

Upon returning to our home, he talks about me with the female caregiver, and she also looks at me in amazement and shows a very loving and proud face to me. I am very tired, but this is a good feeling of tired, not like the old days. When I sleep now, I can close my eyes, and though there are strange noises, I learn of each and that every new discovery brings no reason to remain alert.

"Linda, take a look at this!" Mike said as he removed the data from his GPS, which just spent a rowdy romp through the nearby forest on Sam's collar.

Linda took a look at the graph, colored to show variances in speed. The color bar pointed at 45 mph. A silent question showed on her brow.

Mike replied quickly, "Sam chased a jackrabbit during the hike today, and that's how fast he was going when he caught up to it."

"Amazingly fast little pup," was all Linda could reply. She was quite pleased with his ability, as was Mike. This was only the beginning of their surprise at his capabilities, as time would show, and also the beginning of a wonderful relationship for all three involved parties.

The Visitor in the Night

Both caregivers make a strange noise when they are asleep. It is rhythmic and helps me to sleep myself. The two of them, however, do not share my ability to sleep through noises of a known origin.

First one awakens, and then the other, resulting from a bit of prodding from the one who was awakened by the other. They take turns waking each other, and each time I am awakened by this activity, I remind myself of the harsh ways I was awakened and the fear I had while living on the outside.

Their rhythmic behavior comforts me in a way I have never experienced. It even helps me to try and forget the strong feeling of a spirit which lives here with us. The spirit is of one who looks like my mother and has not yet decided to go to the other side. I hear the jingling but see nothing as I hear it travel from room to room, and then it goes away.

One time, both caregivers awoke and looked in the direction of the jingling. I was relieved to know it is not just me who hears this noise. They were alarmed, especially after looking at me and realizing the jingling was in another area of the home. None of us slept very well that night. The next day, the male caregiver took me to a place I had never been. It was a great hiking place, though smaller in area than my first place.

In this place, there was a very nice canyon, with high rocks on each side. As we approached the convergence of the high rocks, I scented something that had recently left our world. We approached a mound of large rocks, and I knew who was here in this place.

I sensed her presence, and she came to me, jingling. She looked like my mom, though I could see through her to the rocks beyond. She made peace with me that day, and each time after that, when she visited our home, I watched and listened as she walked the empty halls and felt sad for her absence. She felt happy for me, and also happy for the caretaker pair who let me into their lives and home. I thanked her for allowing me to take over this life of hers, which was cut short.

The jingling came back, though less frequently each moon, until after twelve moons had passed. Thereafter, it finally never came back. To this day, I still miss her, but I know she has a new home on the other side, and she is finally at rest. I finally get it, why I am here, and I owe everything to this wonderful creature, as she spawned the feelings within the caregivers that helped them to understand and love me as one of their own.

Now sleep comes easily, and I am comforted by the love of this pack leader and his mate. I now have a real home.

Sam Sleeping on Couch

CHAPTER 4

Sam Has a Discussion with Coyotes

Sam now had quite a large following of canine friends. He became aware of how he should behave in their company so that they didn't fear him or want to attack him. They quickly learned that though Sam never started a fight, he was more than capable of finishing one, and that it was not possible for them to ever prevail in a discussion of this nature without his complete consent.

Often, he would allow a smaller dog to drag him around on the ground and play with him for hours. He would always be praised by his caregivers for such positive behavior, and he actually liked to be the punching bag in play. However, when the play turned into something else, Sam made it very clear to the aggressor exactly who was in control.

This day, several caregivers and their pets would find out that Sam had another side, one which fell hidden beneath his soft fur and curly tail, and one which perked up his ears and allowed his full energy and speed to become apparent.

The day started with a group hike in the area within which his dad and half-siblings live; it was lush with high vegetation and lots of places for rabbits to call home. He was teaching several unleashed fellows how to sneak up on various indigenous residents, though he always obeyed his caregiver's requests to resume the hike. This hike took a steep upward swing of nearly five hundred feet in elevation gain, allowing a remarkable view of the underlying area. It is from here that Sam first saw the coyote pack tracking them below on the hiking trail.

Sam positioned himself for a good view of the activities below, and one by one, the dogs came to see what he was watching. He had a crowd around him when the first caregivers finally climbed the last rocks between them and the canine crowd.

Jeannie was the first human to catch up to the group of pups, which consisted of Sam, a golden that belonged to her, Carl's pound puppy, and Ed's precocious yellow Lab. She gasped in alarm when she saw the object of curiosity the pups were reviewing.

"Get up here, guys. You gotta see this!" she squeaked. Jeannie was rather small and squeaky, as small humans normally are. "Get up here now!" she finished her dialogue.

The humans massed on the hill, each curious at Jeannie's alarming behavior—at least until they each, in turn, looked below.

By now, the group of six coyotes noticed the activity above and began calling out. At the first howl, Sam dropped off the cliff and headed toward the group. The other dogs, upon insistence from their caregivers, took up positions behind and near the caregivers as the fearful humans grabbed for collars and held fast their pets.

Ed scrambled over Jeannie and grabbed at two collars, while Carl stood transfixed by the sight.

"They're just standing there!" Carl said as he watched the coyotes below. "What if they come up here? Does anyone have a gun or something?"

"Yes, and we won't need it," Mike replied as he came over for a closer look. "They won't be coming up here."

As Mike spoke those words, the coyotes were selecting their target from the pups above. They were all looking at the plump golden retriever.

Jeannie, Carl, and Ed grabbed their pups by the collars and forced them to remain on the hill. Mike watched as Sam dropped into the group of predators below. Somehow, Mike knew that Sam was the only one in control here.

Sam knew this group. The Others had been an antagonistic part of his young existence for the last two years and more, and it was time to have a discussion with them about how things were going to be from now on. They were slow learners and occasionally needed a refresher course on behavior. As he descended the cliff, Sam took careful inventory, and by the time he was in their presence, he once again recognized the boss. And as quick as you can snap your fingers, he had the pack leader running for his life.

"Mike, where's Sam going?" Jeannie called out. "I think he's going down there!"

Jeannie was right. The group watched as Sam hurtled to the flat below—exactly where the predators were massing.

Carl finally had a collar in his hand, and the three humans had their charges under control. As they watched the events below, no one spoke and everyone listened. None of them watched Mike, who also watched the events transpire but did not share their concerns. This had happened before, and Mike knew the outcome was not going to be tragic, except for the coyotes.

Yes, the event played out as often before. Sam approached the group, and one coyote stood apart from the Others. It was this fellow that Sam took to the carpet with a huge lunge. The big fellow rolled several times on the ground, and just before he came to his feet, Sam positioned himself over his smaller opponent. The lead coyote remained on the ground and would not make eye contact with Sam as Sam walked over and around him.

Finally Carl spoke, "He just attacked the big one. Where did the other ones go? Are they coming up here?"

Everyone watched as Sam disrupted the meeting below by delivering a strong blow to the chairman. To everyone watching, it was clear that Sam was in control. This did not immediately transfer to a level of comfort for the viewers because they still didn't know where the remaining coyotes were lurking.

"There they go!" Ed observed as he sighted movement in the brush below the knoll on which Sam and the boss were having their discussion. "They're running away, down the hill."

Sam looked like a wild animal. His hair doubled in volume, and he looked as if someone had attached an air hose to him and pumped him up to double size. He looked more like a male lion than a coyote hybrid, and right now, the male coyote beneath him was in fear of his life.

As this was unfolding, the other coyotes disappeared into the brush. They wanted nothing to do with this new stranger, and as coyotes often do, they ran away once again to hunt another day. After a minute or so, Sam allowed the big male to slowly arise, and he also allowed him to leave without harm. Sam climbed back to the ledge where everyone held fast to their companions and went on with his hike just like nothing had happened.

"I can't believe what just happened," Carl offered as he reluctantly released his pup. "How did Sam know who to jump on? How did he know the rest of them wouldn't grab him and eat him?"

"He thinks like a coyote, and like a dog too," Mike clarified. "Sam knows what they are planning to do before they can mass, and because he thinks so much like them, he knows how to pick out the alpha male and rushes him in order to disrupt the attack pattern. It's just that simple. He's done it before, and he'll do it each time he sees them, until they leave him alone."

It was several minutes before all of the humans above allowed their pups to rejoin Sam in his adventures. Only after the coyotes began chastising the group from a distant hill were the humans satisfied there would be no further conflict with this group.

Needless to say, the caregivers began a detailed discussion about how Sam had handled the Others, each giving their take on the situation. Though they still carefully watched their respective pups, there was a significantly lower state of alarm being emitted from each caregiver. It seemed they were taking comfort in Sam's presence as never before, and though each one feared the Others in their own way, the general consensus became that wherever they went, whenever they were planning to hike, they wanted Sam included in the group.

The hike continued, Sam leading the way for the first mile or two, and then, finally, the other pups began to relax and join the search for new and exciting adventures. One found a snake, and Sam pushed the young golden away from it, just in case the snake had a surprise for her. She willingly accepted Sam's suggestion to withdraw, though in her heart, she wanted to either play with or eat the interesting creature.

Sam's Take on the Incident

"I think I'm going to enjoy today," Sam thought to himself as the day began at home with the promise of a long hike with some of his canine friends.

I can't speak, being born without the gift of verbal articulation; however, I can easily make my needs and desires known, though my gentle gestures must often be made repeatedly for the caregivers to understand my needs and intentions. They are slow learners, unlike me, and are not extremely unlike the domesticated canines with which I make company. If I had opposable thumbs, I would be the one writing this book.

Some of my friends know who I am, and most of the Others quickly became aware of me as well—both sides of me, that is. Both of these groups concern themselves primarily with their short-term wants such as food and . . . well . . . food.

On that subject, I am more likely to skip a meal in lieu of having too much on my lean bones to allow me swift and effective response to potential attacks by either group. I'm a thinker, and I spend much of my time wondering about the world around us. I believe that I share that behavior with the humans. It is my cognitive skills that allow me to determine what an errant pack of coyotes is thinking even before they know.

The friends who know me well also realize I am a very quick learner—both of their ways and those of the caregivers. I showed one of them how to open doors and cabinets, and to my chagrin, they quickly relayed the information to their caregiver, who seemed to know exactly where the new skills originated, and once again, I was in trouble.

The memory of being in trouble quickly passed once we began to prepare for today's adventure. My caregiver (who calls himself "Mike") tucked me into the motive device (which he calls "the jeep"), and off we went to meet the other caregivers and their canine companions.

My excitement is apparent as we approach the place where my father was born and still resides. I will try to find him once again as we make way over and through the vegetation, rocks, and hills in this remarkable place. Water is nearby, but we won't be going in that direction. The Others are here too. I can smell them and hear them in the distance. They know of us as well, and once we began to hike, some of them start to follow.

As we start to climb, I lose scent of the Others. We are into the wind, but I can still hear the noisy ones in their small pack below who have not yet learned to travel silently like me. The nearby canines and their caregivers also make a tremendous amount of noise, but even though this impairs my hearing, I can still tell we are being followed.

I entertain my pack with gifts of insight on how to behave in my environment. When they question my suggestions, I sign to them: "I live here, this is my world!" and they understand.

As we round a bush moving at ten times the fastest caregiver's speed, I see food. The most alert of the canines feels my excitement and follows as closely as he can.

We pair off and nearly catch a small rabbit, which chooses cactus punctures in lieu of imminent consumption and lives to play another day.

Moments later, I hear the Others again and assess their position. They are giving us much leeway as we romp and play on the hill just above the six potential aggressors. Two are below us near the caregiver path, and four are under us and to our left.

As long as they remain apart and don't get any closer, I'll allow them to do what comes natural for the Others. After all, this is where they live, and as long as they do not pose a threat to us, they can come and go as they please.

We began a short ascent, with the caregivers somewhat behind us. I climb a small tree after a chipmunk, and the canines circle around on the ground below me, very excited but unable to climb like me. The chipmunk drops behind me and runs to a neighboring tree with the canines in hot pursuit.

Even with this racket all around me, I sense and then see the Others circling below. They are now more interested than before, and I feel they will select one of the canines for the evening meal, and this is unacceptable to me. They begin to talk among themselves, seemingly unconcerned about my detection of their presence.

As the first caregiver reaches us, a small female climbing

slightly ahead of my caregiver, I select my target, the alpha coyote male, and drop from the tree line just as the coyote group's singing starts. The group of six is calling for reinforcements, and the call is answered at the same time I descend from the height toward the Others. Now is the time to send a message, loud and clear, to my old nemesis and his followers. I race toward them with speed unmatched in their range of understanding.

Before the Others can react, I am with them. My caregiver is watching, and the other caregivers are gathering up their canines out of fear that they might join me. There is no room for canine behavior here, and I have shifted to my other self—the one who is stronger, faster, and smarter than the Others and, of course, any canine alive.

The Others have long feared this meeting, and because they failed to eliminate me while I was small and helpless, they now have to experience the consequences of their huge mistake. I focus my aggressive attention on the boss and put him on the ground hard as the remainder of the coyote pack start to back away from the two of us. The one who was so intent on eliminating me is now the submissive one, and he cowers below my angry jaws as I utter a sound so terrible that the remaining five others run from the area. My furry coat appears to grow in thickness, as does my already-full tail, and I seem to double in size. The boss of the Others has resigned himself to a quick death.

I turn away from the boss, leaving him lying there in a state of fear the likes of which he has never experienced. From this day forward, this coyote leader knows he should never try anything with me again, and for the first time since I was adopted by my caregiver, when I hear his singing in the early hours of the night, I will sleep without fear. I hope he remembers this lesson because if he does not, he will not like the consequences.

I trot back up the small hill and over to my caregiver, who

seems very relieved that I have dispatched the Others, as are the remaining caregivers. There is a significant amount of caregiver noise as we continue our hike, and I know from the actions of the caregivers that they wish me to be a part of all future endeavors in this area.

The canines are in awe of my actions. They tell me this by their submissive behavior and the attention which they give me. I know, from today on, that I will have lots of company with me on future hikes.

Sam in Red Tank Draw Wash

CHAPTER 5

Even Sam knows his unique place in society today, thanks in part to a visit from several Hopi artists. It is customary for artists from each of the Hopi, Zuni, and Dine' clans to pay an occasional visit to the native-only store in which Linda once worked. One of these visits introduced Sam to the group of Hopi called the Coyote Clan.

Sam and the Hopi Coyote Clan

Here in Arizona, we are privileged to live close to several Indian groups. Northeast of us is the Navajo Nation or Dine' as they prefer to be called. Dine' means "The People." The Navajo Nation is a sovereign nation, which basically means that they are self-governed. They are located inside the United States, but they are not governed by the laws of the United States.

The Navajo Nation is about sixteen million acres in size and resides in Arizona, Utah, Colorado, and New Mexico, taking up about 25 percent of northeastern Arizona. The Hopi are governed by the Hopi tribal council and are located within the Navajo Nation.

Having worked at an old established store selling Indian goods,

I have made many Navajo friends. The Dine' are a warm, friendly people who earned my respect early on and possess a sense of humor far beyond my expectations.

Though I have collected jewelry and pottery from many different tribes, my favorite pieces are the ones I bought directly from the artist. Knowing the artist who fashioned my pieces makes it more personal for me and for the artist. Because of my passion, he or she knows that I will wear the art and appreciate it for many years to come.

For some reason, the earthy, honest feel of the Navajo work talks to me, and I can feel the heart of the artist when I wear it. My second favorite form of artwork is the silver overlay done by the Hopi. It is clean and exact. A piece of silver is etched and then darkened with an acid, and then the patterned piece (cutout) is placed on top. This creates a wonderfully weighty piece.

Figures of animals and crops dominate many of the pieces as well as representations of weather, rain, wind, lightning, and clouds. Most of the pieces I saw in the store had the clan of the artist on the back, or underside, of the piece instead of those being signed with initials or names like the Navajo.

Hopi is made up of a system of "villages" occupying three mesas. Walpi is the oldest village, located on First Mesa and was originally established in about 1690. Some Tewa also live on First Mesa. They came to find peace and comfort when the Spanish waged war on them for refusing to accept their Christian doctrine. According to a Hopi friend, they were allowed to live here on one condition. "You and your people can come in, but you must take all the ugly women."

It is believed that some contact with Europeans was made in the sixteenth century. Some Spanish missions were built in Hopi villages starting in 1629 and were in operation until the Pueblo Revolt of 1680, which drove the Spanish out of their Pueblo. Of all the Pueblo tribes, it was the Hopi who kept them out permanently. Regular contact with the whites did not occur again for two more centuries, thus keeping their spiritual belief system pure.

The Hopi also live on Second Mesa and Third Mesa. About 2,300 square miles belong to the Hopi, who number about seven thousand as of the most recent census. Archaeological records show that prehistoric agriculture was introduced to the southwest as early as 1500 BC by the Anasazi, ancestors of the Hopi, who built sophisticated agricultural civilizations in many of the areas of the Southwest. Evidence gathered from pictographs and petroglyphs suggest that the occupation of the American Indian and their methods of survival, hunting, and farming predate the pyramids of Egypt.

Back to the Coyote Clan

On a windy day in February, there were several artists coming by to see the buyer at the store. The buying days had changed, and those of us who worked that day had the unobstructed delight in seeing what they brought. It was going to be an expensive day.

We had all tried on our new purchases and approved of the new "needed" accessories, and it was getting close to time to close the door when several things happened. First, three Hopi artists came in wanting to sell. We started talking. I knew from previous meetings that they were from the Coyote Clan of Hopi. Then my husband Mike and Sam came in. They were on their way home from visiting a local nursing home and decided to come by to see Mommy.

My Hopi friends were taken aback when they saw Sam. One exclaimed, "He is one funny-looking coyote!" We explained how we came to find Sam, how he had found lost children and dogs, and how he saved me when I fell from the mountain. They were so impressed by the story of Sam that they wanted to honor him by making him a member of their clan.

They unwrapped their velvet rolls containing pieces of jewelry and removed a pendant. On the front of the pendant was a coyote. They said some things in their Hopi (Uto-Aztecan) language and placed the pendant on Sam's collar. He was now an honorary member of the Coyote Clan.

From that day forward, he seemed to hold his head a little higher. He knew an honor had been bestowed upon him. He now had a new job to do, and that was to spread the Coyote Clan tradition to both humans and their canine companions. A few notes follow regarding the clan.

*"Ishauu" or Coyote Clan

The coyote was a symbol or totem of the Hopi Coyote Clan and Water Coyote Clan. The coyote knew the path to those in the spirit world; he could see into the past and the future. He had the power to call down lightning and the power to heal.

Throughout the ages, the coyote has become well known for his survivability in harsh environments and also has become both feared and respected by the humans who both share and encroach on his environment.

Sam shares this knowledge and adds to it his knowledge of the canine side, as taught him by his numerous canine friends. Though living in both worlds has its challenges, Sam as acclimated to this dual lifestyle and shares his knowledge and experience with friends on both sides of the fence.

Sam's Hopi Coyote Clan Pendant

CHAPTER 6

Sam's First Few Days and First Time with a Babysitter

Sam was beginning to learn the ropes in this new environment, where it seemed to him he had much more latitude in behavior and significantly more love and respect. Given this, Sam wandered through his new environment daily, presumably looking for escape routes and secretly marking territory.

We found out months later that he had done this marking thing, and we quietly cleaned up after him. He was aware of this and appreciated us all the more. This is the first time in his young life that he didn't get chastised for being himself, so he was quick to adjust to the new living arrangement, and he received love and rewards in return for good behavior.

We know it makes absolutely no sense to punish a canine for something he did many weeks or months ago because he has long forgotten the incident and would have absolutely no action on which to reference the punitive measures. Besides, we never punish, anyway. We were blessed that he didn't feel the need to repeat this marking process.

Special note: Black lights are wonderful detection tools in identifying this situation.

Sam always seemed to be most comfortable outdoors. When we brought him home, I spent a day extending the height of the wall that surrounds our dog run to a height of over six feet, knowing of Sam's tendency to leap tall buildings in a single bound.

He watched me work on the wall while sunning himself and seemed OK with my actions. He talked with me on occasion, presumably helping me address how straight and true my handiwork was becoming and how unnecessary the changes were.

It turns out that this attempt to make the wall tall enough to dissuade Sam's scaling capabilities was a wasted effort for two reasons. Sam wasn't interested in leaving once he spent the first week in his new home and became acclimated. The other reason became apparent the first time a pack of coyotes came through the neighborhood, presumably looking for someone's cat or little dog left unattended.

Sam heard their calling, waited until they were very close, and went through the doggie door and over the wall without even touching it. He ran toward the pack at very high speed, scattering them to the four winds, and slowly trotted back, over the wall, and then parked himself on the bed near Linda. We had awakened the moment he exited the doggie door, and by the time I was outside and looking for him, he had rescaled the wall, reentered the home, and rejoined Linda in bed. I walked back into the room surprised to see him there, but happy he returned so quickly. So much for the wall-too-high theory.

Sam

I walk through this new place and make it my own with scent. The scent does not remain for long, as my caregivers remove it, but they do not take displeasure in my actions like other caregivers did before. Since they do not like it, I decide to discontinue this action.

I have discovered when I do something which pleases my caregivers, that they treat me exceptionally well and often reward me for not doing things that require additional actions from them. I am very perceptive, and I immediately know if I have acted in a manner that does not conform.

Though I intend to retain my individuality, I also want to walk a path that my caregivers prefer, so I watch and learn from them. They never punish me, as so many others before them have, and always reward me with gifts and attention when I am good. This behavior is new and very pleasurable for me.

I have learned from patrolling the area I now call home where every exit is and where every entry point is located. I save this information in case it is needed, as it was several times before among other humans while I was growing.

I feel that it will not be necessary to leave this place, but just in case it is, I will have the capability to do so. I will never again be restrained or kept from being free, as has happened too many times before. It is not in my nature to be completely domesticated.

My caregiver is carefully making an enclosure, which protects us from the outside. I watch as he performs this task, and he seems to enjoy my company. He has increased the height of the enclosure, though this change does not affect my capability to exit should I deem it necessary, so he must be doing this to keep other creatures outside.

I occasionally hear the Others talking outside the wall, and I am comforted by his desire to protect me from them. His efforts are very comforting to me, as I know from experience that a coyote never jumps down into an area which they do not believe they can safely and quickly exit. I am certain my caretaker knows this as well.

One day, the Others come too close, and I hear them. My

caregivers are making the sleeping noise and cannot hear them, so it is up to me to discuss their proximity with them and suggest an alternative location within which they will be allowed to do their business.

I exit through the moving door, and over the wall I go. Within seconds, I am among the Others, and since this has happened before and the results did not favor them, they quickly disperse north toward the hills and beyond. I hear them calling back to me in anger, knowing that I will not pursue them to this place. I return to my caregivers, who are now awake and watching me curiously as I lie down to sleep. Tomorrow I will pick a perching place inside this wonderful place so that I can better track movements of things both inside and outside.

Sam spent one entire afternoon trying out each chair in the living room. He decided on the one that allowed him a view down the hall, a view of the front door, and the best view of the red rocks to the north. We bought him a nice cushioned cover for the chair, and he adopted it for his own. To this day, we remind visitors to leave that chair available, unless they want an eighty-pound lapdog to accompany them.

Sam knows where everything is. He has several cupboards in the home for his treats and food and has the rest of his stuff scattered throughout—his stuff being dog cookies, bully sticks, extra toys, shampoo, brushes, and whatever new thing catches our eye with him in mind.

After dinner, if he is still wanting, he goes to the cupboard, decides on what he wants, and he herds one of us over to the area and points at the desired object. All of us know that if we don't give him what he asks for, he retains the option of opening the cabinet and grabbing it himself. He has yet to exercise that option, however.

To recap: Everything is in reach; he could just take what he wants, but he never does. When we are absent, he never takes anything by himself. I also feel he has created this discipline for himself in order not to cause us any displeasure.

I believe firmly that if there were two canines in the household, everything we know of him would change, and there would be a doggie party, and upon detection of the events and missing stuff by one of us, I'm certain each canine would point at the other as the perpetrator of the incident. I'm also convinced that there would be a marking party and a very empty water dish upon our return.

I am also pretty sure that if we had two pets, one of them just might become part of the food chain, and I'm positive that one would definitely not be Sam. He does not like to share.

Linda's Take

Sam had no clue.

Sam had no clue how to be a dog. He knew how to be free—to hunt and play and run and chase the other creatures in the forest. He knew how to kill only enough to eat in order to survive. He respected the normal balance of things. This was the free Sam. As a dog leased out to caretakers (at least, until he found us), he knew only how to be chained in a yard, ignored, and how to be left alone and heartbroken.

When we brought Sam home, it was late afternoon. We tried to feed him dog food interlaced with chicken, and he was not at all interested. I washed the dog door flap so he could see through it, and he used it with no difficulty.

He wanted nothing to do with it until he could see what was on the other side. Once it was clean, he exited and did his business and came back inside, went straight to our bed, and jumped up, moving around until he found the best spot. He slept through the night. In the morning, he woke up with us, tail wagging.

I made my decision at that moment. If he used the doggie door and slept through the night, anything else could be taught. We were keeping him.

The next day, we tried to play ball with him. The ball hit him on the nose; he let it roll away. Okay, we can learn this. Once Sam gets the idea, there is no stopping him. Mike put his hand under the covers one morning and tried to get Sam's foot. Sam went straight up in the air and ran to the guest room and hid under the bed. The next time, he nearly gave Mike stitches. He had learned the game and was playing for keeps.

This was to be the case with all the games and toys we tried. It took a little time, but with affectionate reassurance, he not only learned but was proud of his accomplishments. If we tried to take a nap, he would stand over us and wait for us to open our eyes. If that didn't work, he would drop a toy on our chest. We loved him and his puppylike behavior. We felt we were making progress.

Over time, with a daily trip to the forest so Sam could be a coyote, we finally found the right balance. It took a good six months of trial and error, but he settled in.

One of the things we noticed, though subtle, was the way he slept. Gradually, he began to sleep more soundly and for longer periods of time. Finally, we would see him on the bed flat on his back really sound asleep. Surely, in the wild, he had never been allowed to feel this safe. We were actually becoming a pack. Now it was time for us to learn each other's pack behaviors.

Now it was also time for Sam to teach his dog friends how he lives and what to do in order to stay on his good side. Dogs have the tendency to test the fences in the pecking order. Where Sam is concerned, this behavior just might not achieve the same result, as will be discussed later.

Sam is an expert at controlling and using the pecking order.

It is one thing that he inherited from his father, and in the coyote world, violation of the pecking order can and often does result in elimination of the offending party. The wild part of him, mixed with the strength and confidence he derived from his mother's side, allow Sam a lot of latitude in determining his position.

Inviting the Outside In

Sam had been left alone for most of the late afternoon and evening. He was still in puppy stage even though he was twenty months old. He was getting more comfortable with staying home and entertaining himself. He spent most of his time outside sunning and playing with his many toys.

When we got home, we were tired, having spent the last four hours at a major artist's showing. So many friends, so many glasses of wine, so many hours with a frozen smile, so many hours just standing around . . . we were pooped!

When we opened the door, we were greeted by a tail wagging so hard it was going in circles. Kisses for all and a quick check of his water and dry food supply and it's time for bed.

By the time we had changed our clothes, Sam was comfortably curled up on the foot of the bed.

Sometime after midnight, Sam stealthily poured himself off the foot of the bed. I thought I heard a peep, but I was tired and needed sleep. Sam sounded like he was playing, so we went back to sleep with earplugs added.

The next day was like any other. Sam, however, was lying in front of the china cabinet, eyes wide open and seemingly guarding something. Another peep! And more peeps! I called Sam out and put him in the bathroom until I could do a little investigating.

I got down on the floor and took a peek. Oh my gosh! Out they came. There were at least a dozen of them. Them being baby quail. Soon, running walnuts were going every which way like a handful of ball bearings.

Okay, time for assistance. I called Mike, and we ran around with dishtowels, herding little ones out whichever door was open and relatively close. We were pretty sure we got them all, but with the constant "peeping," it was hard to know who was in and who was out. Sam, of course, yipped at decibels loud enough to hurt one's ears.

Once these little ones were outside, we needed to collect them in one area and hope Mom and Dad would recognize their voices and come collect their little charges. Once that was done, it was time to let Sam out of the bathroom and discuss what does and does not belong *inside* the house.

Of course, this caused looks of confusion and tilting of his head, along with a yip that said he was not going to get this at all. Another peep! This one he found before we did. These were his playmates—*his*! We let him and his playmate outside and hoped for no more peeps inside.

It was Mike who found the next uninvited houseguest. During the night, Mike thought he heard something in the bathroom. He turned the light on and began to look in the snail shower, the potty room, the closet—nothing. The sound returned, and this time, Mike thought he saw something move.

Gopher! Needless to say, there were way too many people in too small a space to catch the critter. Sam decided to join in the fun. With all the bumping into each other and Sam thinking it was playtime, our gopher disappeared. I went into the kitchen to get a glass of cold water and saw something move. I was just about to call Mike when he yelled, "I got the son of a gun."

Oh s——!

Exactly how many "friends" did Sam invite to move in?

The second one was easier to catch, and we reluctantly deduced that there were only two.

LEAPING LIZARDS and the list goes on.

Our first clue was finding a tail without a lizard. The second was hearing Sam scurrying around on the tile floor in the middle of the night.

Give me a break; my son not only got up in the night but also turned on the TV.

Apparently not.

Lizards come in all sizes and colors, and over time, we have seen them all—inside, outside, stashed in shoes. Sam is amazing, but he has no clue who belongs inside and who belongs outside.

It reoccurs to me slowly that Sam is an outdoor animal who actually lived outside before we let him live in the house. He can't process our logic because it makes no sense to him. If he can live outside and inside, why can't they?

Okay, we need to rethink the rules.

Anytime we see him coming in with a "friend," we ask him to "leave it" outside—and he does. Occasionally when we move furniture, we find a deceased "friend," but the practice in general has quieted down immensely.

Sam's Spider Pet

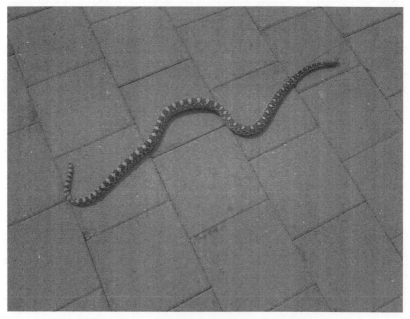

Sam's Snake Pet

CHAPTER 7

People Food

We were determined not to *ever* give Sam people food. Almost never . . . Well, sometimes . . .

When we brought Sam home, he was very thin. His bones stood out all over his body. His head and his feet seemed huge, but there was this uncanny tail that looked like it belonged in a show ring. We tried brand after brand of dog food to no avail. We knew he had to eat, so we tried a little chicken. That worked! We mixed it with the dry, and he ate the chicken out of the bowl and left the dry.

The experiment begins. Doesn't like fish, chips, french fries, sausage, milk, cold cereal, hot cereal, cheese, ham, roast beef, bananas, carrots, celery, eggs—the list goes on.

He does like hot dogs, hamburger, chicken, noodles, chicken chow mein, peanut butter, and ice cream. The ice cream experiment happened one night after dinner when we had vanilla bean ice cream with chocolate sauce for dessert. Sam came to beg, showing signs of our family's obsession with ice cream, although he didn't know what it was or why he wanted it.

Mike put a large spoonful in a small bowl and set it on his favorite chair.

Sam sniffed and sniffed again, finally putting his nose on the cold white confection. The moment was legendary; a small experimental lick, then lots of licks until the serving was small enough to swallow whole. Sam's looking at us with overwhelming love and appreciation was followed by Sam rubbing his head on the oriental carpet, around and around. Brain freeze!

When the pain subsided, he asked for more. We had created an ice cream addict.

On one of the days we were introducing him to the other dogs in the neighborhood at the dog park, Cindy, Ellie's mom, was giving little treats to the other dogs. Sam was given a taste and kept begging for more. She held out her hand and offered the rest. Sam gobbled it up.

Naturally, I ran to ask her, "What is that magic food?" She gave me the name and where to get it. It was an all-natural dog food. I liked that; no more people food.

The next day, Sam and I drove to Cottonwood to the Feed Store. We bought a small bag. When we got home, I made Sam a small dinner with chicken on top. Within seconds, the bowl was clean.

He has been on the same brand of food, changing formulas as needed—especially since he is part wild animal, and he tends to try to "fatten up" when fall arrives.

We still mix some chicken in his food on occasion, so the quail and rabbits who play on the property can visit with safety.

We are so grateful that Cindy came to the rescue, but her golden retriever Ellie is just a pain as far as Sam is concerned. She is a beautiful creature who loves Sam. Actually, she is obsessed with Sam. Sam is considerably less enthusiastic about her, though.

She won't leave him alone. She runs whining toward Sam when

he arrives at the dog park, and she rolls over on her back and begs for attention. She kisses him and body slams him and slobbers all over him.

Mike says that's the way I acted when we first met, but I doubt it.

Sam Talking With Ellie

CHAPTER 8

Flipping the Coin

We were not completely ready for what was to come. Within a week of adopting Sam, Mike had to go to San Diego on business. He was gone over a week, and the change in Sam's behavior was dramatic. This could go either way, just like a coin toss.

As soon as Mike left, Sam began to panic. I tried to take him out in the yard to play, brushing him, even enticing him with treats. He wanted nothing to do with any of it. He kept looking over the wall; I was sure he would bolt.

He refused to eat or sleep. He paced the house and whined. My heart was broken. He was sure he had been abandoned. The second night, he slept by the door in the laundry room that led to the garage. The third night, he slept with me. The pack leader behavior kicked in.

Sam never left my side. We hiked together side by side instead of him going off to chase anything that moved. He was at my feet every minute of the day and night. If I got up in the night, he was there. Even when he was eating, I didn't dare leave because he would follow me.

This would sound sweet if it wasn't for his posturing. He stood between me and any access to me, sharp and alert. He was guarding one of his pack. This wasn't play to him; he didn't even want to hug or be petted. It was work; it was his new job.

When Mike returned, I told him all about Sam, and though surprised, he was pleased by the new behavior. We were about to find out that his new behavior ranged way beyond guarding.

The next time we went for a hike, Sam felt I was in good hands with Mike, so he trotted off to be the coyote Sam. We always knew approximately where he was and also that he would come back to us, and he always did. This time, however, was different. Off he went after something, swiftly running through the bushes. Calling his name was absolutely ineffective. Finally, he returned on his own, thank goodness.

In his mouth was a good-sized rabbit, which he laid at Mike's feet. Okay, this is nice, but what to do next? Do we scold or praise? Praise won out, and he was so proud. He was the leader of our pack and was providing for us.

We began to walk again. Sam picked up the rabbit and followed. His job was done. He and his catch parted ways at the jeep. We had already resigned ourselves to having a rabbit dinner to prepare for Sam's dinner that evening; however, we were spared. He stashed the rabbit beneath some cactus and rejoined us as we walked toward the trailhead above.

There were more hikes and more offerings. Meanwhile, Sam was beginning to change his behavior toward birds and rabbits in our yard, particularly becoming protective toward the quail and other birds in his yard. We could almost see his brain working. These were *his* birds and *his* quail. When the rabbits came in to eat from the bird dish, his body would begin to shake, and a whine could be heard. Once in a while, he would take undertake a chase, only to be reminded that he was not to leave the boundaries of the yard. He would chase the rabbit to the edge of the yard and stop just before exiting our property.

On the next hike to the forest, Sam and Mike went without me. At the end of the hike, Sam brought Mike a quail. Mike knew it was gone, but he saw the look on Sam's face. He didn't mean to hurt the bird. Mike reassured Sam that the bird was okay, and Sam's tail began to wag again.

Mike tossed the bird up into a tree and prayed it would hang up on a branch and stay there. It did, and both of the boys went home happy. The next morning, Sam went to the very spot Mike had performed the bird-toss. Fortunately, something had already carried it off, presumably thankful we left it a convenient meal.

The Trip

One day, Linda and I had to be where Sam was not. We were concerned because, until now, at least one of us had been present all the time. Though Sam had well acclimated to his surroundings, he still was concerned about change, as change seemed to disrupt his lifestyle and mandate unwanted behavior alterations.

Sam was rapidly becoming less jittery every day, but he wasn't entirely pensive, however, and his first experience without both of us nearby was pretty interesting. Before this event, we worked on various plans of how we would introduce him to our absence. It was Mike's turn first to be away for a few days, so we performed an experiment to see how Sam would behave.

Up until now, Sam hadn't made very many sounds. No barking at the mailman, dogs, cars, or asking for food or treats by begging. He was stealthy and tentative in everything he did, and he was not willing to eat with us present.

Even when he ate with us cautiously viewing him, he would drag his food from the bowl and position himself so he could watch us while he ate. I found out later that this behavior is common in predatory animals feeding in the wild. They remove their food from the kill site so they couldn't be ambushed while eating.

I went outside into the garage and could hear him near the door. He sniffed at the door and then began to yip not unlike a coyote pup. When I opened the door, he flattened his ears and stood looking at me. I closed the door, and it began again.

We went through this activity three more times. Finally, he decided to lie against the door where he could hear me outside and was finally satisfied I wasn't going to leave him. Thereafter, he was OK with me going outside.

We did the same for Linda, and as long as one of us was there, he was fine.

The day came, however, when we both need to be somewhere else. Our neighbor offered to watch Sam while we ventured off for a day. Sam knew him from several visits, so we felt he would be a good companion for Sam. What happened was the most interesting bit of behavior from Sam we had experienced until now.

Dan took his favorite chair in the living room. Sam sat in front of him. While Dan read a magazine, Sam made guttural sounds and stared at Dan, adding in an occasional yip. When Dan stood up, Sam would walk over to the garage door and stare back and forth between the very puzzled Dan and the inanimate door.

Dan tried treats, food, water, and anything else that came to mind to dissuade Sam from this behavior, finally deciding to have a talk with Sam. Dan explained to Sam that his behavior was questionable at best, and he admitted to Sam that he was acting pretty scary.

Sam seemed to accept the discussion and replied by taking a chair opposite Dan, still watching his every move but finally giving Dan the gift of silence.

The rest of Dan's stay was uneventful, fortunately, for both Dan and Sam. When we returned the following day, Sam was very happy to see us, and since then, he has been the perfect example of proper canine behavior in our absence. Thanks go to Dan for his patience and understanding.

Because of his good behavior, we never plan to take him to a kennel or any other overnight facility. He is prone, as well evidenced by his prior behavior, to become an escape artist; and if this ever happens again, we fear that we might lose him forever.

He is, after all, very adaptable, as Mother Nature has made him. It is also possible, however, that he would value his life with us so much that he would, and probably could, find his way home. As we all know, stranger things have happened in the animal kingdom.

A Look through Sam's Eyes

As I walk through this mystical place, I find the scent of many others who have been here, and I am driven to erase their scent by replacing it with my own. Many of the scents are very old, much older than me, so I fear the owners of the scents might return to find me easy prey. If I eliminate their scent, they will never find me. I seek comfort in this action.

I have found the way outside. A magic panel in one of the glass doors opens at my push. My best times have always revolved on being able to get outside and enjoy the warm sun and hear everything that happens around me. The barrier is high and makes me feel secure, so I can sleep comfortably here.

The gate allows smaller creatures to enter and amuse me. I have a small army of delectable lizards who make sport of coming in, getting my interest, and making for the nearest exit with me close behind. I have learned that eating the whole lizard makes me sick, but if I just eat the tail, I obtain nutrition. And when the lizard grows another, I can repeat the process.

Most of the lizards that pester me have very short tails. The caregivers find amusement in my harvesting lizard tails and are amazed by my resourcefulness. They learn slowly, but they finally get the picture.

My caregiver has made changes to the barrier, making it more difficult for things to come and get me. I understand the barrier is here for my protection, and I am appreciative of this wonderful thing. At night, when everything is still and the caregivers are making a symphony of nasal music, I often cross the barrier to seek the Others who have been taking their kill from the nearby grassy area.

After the first time I crossed the barrier to find the Others, they are less willing to come close enough for me to detect them, as our first encounter did not go well for them. Other creatures have been preying on the Others as well. I have sensed the smell of fear when they are approached by caregivers, and I know from their behavior that some of the other caregivers who inhabit this area have done harm to the Others.

Sometimes I sense fear in various caregivers who see me without my caregiver, and I know they are mistaking me for one of the Others, and I feel sadness for them. They do not know me. I am not one creature, but two, and they fear the one within me that they do not understand. With knowledge comes truth, and truth erases fear, but as I've thought many times before, most caregivers are very slow to learn.

I have no den here, but I have my special places in this home which houses me and the caregivers. I was very careful to choose a place where I had the protection of height and partial visibility of each entry point. In this place, I am able to see and hear everything that happens here.

My place is one of two identical seating areas, and from here, I can see north, south, east, and west and am somewhat difficult to detect upon initial entry. This fact is evidenced by many caregiver visitors who show their surprise upon first sensing me.

There are things in this place which I know are for me alone. The caregivers never touch them unless they are bringing them to me. One is a type of food, and several others are special treats which I ask for and receive routinely. Because of this, I never take without asking, as is my nature when away from here. In this place, I have no need to be stealthy or greedy, and this change in my nature makes me look pretty darned good when I am compared with other canines. Most canines I know will eat until they fall over, and then they get up again and eat more.

I don't always eat every day. I never did while living away from here, or when I was living alone in the place near the water. I see canines that eat every day, and they are slow and lethargic. I emulate their slow and methodical behavior sometimes in their presence—it allows me to blend within the pack, even though I am clearly the obvious leader.

One of my jobs is to keep order in the pack. When we are in the grassy area called the school, I occasionally need to present our pack philosophy (as determined by me) to newcomer canines that are big and controlling.

They always come to me and try to present their opinion; however, after a few quick words and sometimes a bit more from me, they get the message. I allow all of the pack members to treat me as a punching bag as long as they realize when we are through playing, and I make this obvious.

This way, each learns from me the methods of evading injury from all sides and angles, which is the first thing I learned while living alone. Danger never comes from the front; it almost always comes from behind. I, in turn, learn how canines play and attack aggressors: knowledge which has become valuable on several occasions.

When I first arrived, I didn't know the rules. Sometimes the caregivers must leave. I was fearful history was repeating itself when my male caregiver went outside and didn't come right back. I could hear him outside and called to him as I would call to my father and mother.

He came back inside and talked with me for a while and went back outside. We did this for a few times, and I realized he would come back each time, so I decided to lie down just inside the door and patiently wait.

The female caregiver did the same thing, and I knew right away she was testing me, so after the first time, I repeated my process of waiting quietly inside for her return. I knew at once I would not be left alone for a very long time, which is something my previous caretakers often did.

One day, both of them left after talking with me for quite a while. They left Dan here to watch over me. I wasn't happy with this option at all, and I let Dan know. It was clear that Dan didn't appreciate being chastised for being put in this situation, but at first, he said and did nothing.

Finally, after quite a while, he got down on the floor near me and we had a discussion. Both of us had our say, and afterward, I was OK with the situation and finally gave Dan his peace. We both enjoyed the remainder of the evening without further incident, except I had to ask him twice for my ice cream dessert, and he joined me once he understood.

Sam in His Favorite Chair

# CHAPTER 9

Everyone gets a different view of Sam on the first meeting. This rings true for man or beast. Here's some insight on his first few days, weeks, and months with us.

Sam, being a composite of two different personalities, might seem to be a different creature depending on whom, or what, you are and your expectations based on his initial take of you.

If you see his canine side, you are witness to the golden retriever part of his personality, and even though he might not look exactly like one of the kindest breeds of canine you can ever meet, you feel his overflowing compassion and love. This was the first part of Sam we met.

However, if you see the wild one that shares the physical realm with the kind and gentle golden, you come face to face with an untamed spirit which has the capability of reading your mind and anticipating your every move, even before you think things out enough to act.

This spirit came from his father and is the basis for his survival instincts and cognitive skills. Both canine and human beings often see this side of Sam, and both are smart enough to keep this in mind when interacting with him. It was a while before Sam allowed us to witness this side.

Sam adapted well and quickly to our home life, and as things came up which required interaction of him, Sam showed us he was more than capable of becoming who we wanted him to be. Once he became comfortable with us, he began testing the fences, and his personality emerged. This gift to us from Sam helped us out of our personal crises and allowed us to emerge from the month-long hole we dug.

We now had a purpose and reason to continue, and this single gift was greater than the sum of our problems and issues. To this day, we think about where we were, what happened, and where we are now, and we silently give thanks for the miracle of Sam.

And still, to this day, Sam loves to experiment with our latitude.

Today, Sam decided to confide in me his desire for a hot dog. Upon seeing me cook a pair of them for lunch, he found it necessary to distract me into a short trip to the garage. He did this by lowering his head and staring at the door that leads from the laundry room to the garage. Being the concerned type, I quickly went to the garage door, took a short listen, and went outside.

When I returned, one hot dog was missing, and Sam was nowhere to be found. I called to him, and he came from outside, a wry smile on his face. I conceded this one to him, letting him know by my actions that I appreciated his cunning.

Earlier this week, Sam wasn't feeling particularly well and got sick outside. He also had a touch of the softies, prompting me to call for a prescription that would take care of the issue. Sam has become accustomed to asking us for help when he is a bit off, and he is quick to allow us to go through the process of giving him the medication in the customary manner, which means forcing his jaw open and driving the pills down his throat with an index finger.

Though he willingly came to us for the medication, he still deemed it necessary to go through the ritual of making it difficult for us to administer the medication. Though he wants to get better, he doesn't want to concede too easily. Sounds like he picked up this behavior from human nature, doesn't it?

As we became accustomed to Sam and adapted to his needs and wants, it became obvious to me that his strengths could expose him to different forms of danger than most canines are subject to experience. His love of hunting and love of the forest around our home gave him access to dangerous creatures, some of which could do him serious harm. Because of this, I decided to train Sam to be cautious around snakes.

The opportunity to do this came suddenly as I walked down to the mailbox. I found a huge gopher snake lounging in the road, and being the good citizen I am, I quickly removed it from the road.

Rather than letting it go its way in peace, I brought it inside and let Sam have a look. The snake was pretty agitated, and when Sam came near, it grabbed him by the nose and was rapidly transported by Sam through each room in the house before finally letting go of his very agitated snout.

To this day, Sam will not approach a snake, and he often shows me when he finds one, in the hope that I'll make it go away. He has found quite a few rattlesnakes, and because he is cautious in their presence, he is still alive today.

Rabbits are another story. Sam has made many a meal of these tender delicacies. They are fast and cautious around him, but Sam has proven to be faster than the fastest rabbits. Given deep cover, they can evade him; but in the open, they are nothing but moving targets.

When we first got Sam, we were very cautious about letting him run free (for fear he would leave), but once he became accustomed to living with us, we allowed him the freedom he needed to survive. When I realized he was faster than the average canine, I decided to clock him with a GPS attached to his collar.

On a recent hiking experience, he found a jackrabbit to chase and, while in pursuit, obtained a top speed over 45 mph. He was closing on the rabbit who, upon realizing this, decided to obtain the protection of a huge cactus plant. Sam decided to give him the latitude of safety he earned and came back to me, leaving the jackrabbit for another day.

It's another early Monday morning, and Sam has visitors for his walk today. We'll do about six miles with about one thousand feet of elevation gain so Sam and his friends can spend time with deer, elk, rabbits, and the elusive chipmunk.

Two German shepherds, two ridgebacks, and Sam start out after Sam has a discussion with the group so they understand the rules of engagement in his world. Two of the pups are quick to learn, but two need encouragement, so Sam puts them in their place. He has only to have a brief word with them, punctuated by some very quick moves on his part, to get his message across, and then all is well, and the hike begins without further incident.

Sam leads the troupe on an exciting trek through juniper stands, where he shows them the benefit of juniper berries in the diet. In addition, there are some residual manzanita berries around and mesquite beans for dessert. Each of the canines gives the treats a try, and they seem to find them to be quite good, despite the caregivers' concerns. This concern gives way to a greater concern as the coyotes nearby start calling from both sides of the group.

Sam tracks the coyotes as the caregivers round up their brood, but it is all to no avail, as the coyotes pass behind us and leave the area silently. Sam points to them as they make their descent from the mountain and head toward the nearby creek. I think to myself that it is very good they have not interacted with this healthy group of canines and, of course, Sam.

As the hike progresses, it is obvious the canines are taking their behavior clues from Sam who is actively pinging the area for signs of life. He brings out several rabbits, two very creative chipmunks, and a very active pair of deer for the canines to study. All of them show their gratitude to Sam in their own unique way.

About a mile from the cars, Sam finds a coyote's stash, which consists of several small bones and a very nice deer clavicle with meat on it. This starts a feeding frenzy when the canines get wind of the find, and each of them tries to grab it from Sam.

This turns out to be a very bad idea, for each of them gets to see a side of Sam they never wanted to meet but now have to accept. Sam has a discussion with each in turn, and they soon understand that their interest in the prize, however well justified in their minds, is something which they will need to curtail going forward.

Dogs are good learners and have a great memory capacity and retention. This becomes obvious when a canine that has previously met and confronted Sam revisits. The process of learning who is who never has to be reprocessed. On the rare occasion a canine who has met Sam before confronts him, Sam stands his ground, and often, the charging dog slams on his brakes as he approaches, once his limited vision gives him a clear look at Sam.

Occasionally, several dogs become a pack, especially in an environment like a dog park, and together, they try to put one over on Sam. The result is always the same. Sam finds the de-facto leader and puts him on the carpet, and then he polls the remainder to see if there is any reason to repeat the process with them. Seldom is there a second taker.

Many times in play, Sam will appear to be recessive and submissive so that younger or smaller pups can role-play and attack him. Sam enjoys this type of play, unless one of the pups gets too aggressive, upon which Sam will administer a warning. Repeated warnings, if necessary, are a bit more severe, and eventually the pup gets the message.

Sam has done this with me on occasion, when I attempt to do anything which involves his feet. He pulls my hand away, each time a bit more strongly, until I give up or get the job done. He will probably never get his nails clipped because of this behavior. He will probably never need them done if he continues to hike five to ten miles a day, as he does now.

I find this response to my help slowly going away, as Sam understands we are trying to make his life better. He gives us a small bit of time to find the sticker, file away a bit of split nail, or put something on a cut pad or other injury. It is nice to know he will never have to have his nails clipped. As mentioned before, five-mile hikes each morning and an occasional evening walk are good remedies for long nails. If he ever needed his nails clipped, I wouldn't want to be the one elected to the task.

Sam and I are evolving a relationship which allows me to understand his wants and needs, as well as help him understand our lives and how they intertwine. He is a strong and important part of our pack, and because of this, we do things for each other— often without polling one another, since we know what needs to be done. This book is about our relationship and how that relationship makes both of our lives better.

I'm writing this book for Sam. He tells me what to say through actions and whatever perception I have, and I interpret his meaning the best I can. He would write, but he has trouble with attention span, and the keyboard gives him fits. He is jealous of my articulated thumbs, but since he can communicate with me, he finds our relationship a convenient method to get his message heard without him enduring the training or surgery required to make his thoughts into words by other means.

Sometimes I get things wrong, so he reiterates on occasion, which is why the second half of many chapters gives a different viewpoint of various occurrences. I am in touch with his golden half, having been the caregiver of one for many years before this time.

The other half of Sam, upon inspection of my work, often clarifies or changes the thoughts I derive from him into words more consistent with the other's meaning. Thus, two different viewpoints are possible, and a merging of these two viewpoints is the only way to completely understand Sam.

The previous section is my perception of our first few days, weeks, and months together, and the rest of this chapter depicts Sam's viewpoint on the same time frame. He definitely has a strange way of looking at things, as one would expect from a creature with two distinctly different methods of assimilating and processing observations.

Sam's Viewpoint

As I walk among the caregivers, I perceive different thoughts from each of them I encounter. Some welcome me with open arms, as they know a big part of my mother's affection and love lives within me; but some look upon my face and know I am something stronger, more powerful, and the best part of two different beings. This brings fear into their hearts. I can smell fear, and in most cases, I do what I can to change these feelings within them.

I find the caregivers who have canine pets to be more understanding of my uniqueness, and because of this, they convey these feelings to their canines. This makes life easier for all of us—both canine and caregiver. Some canines, however, do not have this level of compassion for their caregivers and form an opinion of their own, and because of my medium size, they often try to make sport of me. This is their biggest mistake, as their behavior causes them to quickly come face to face with the image of my father.

I know from experience to keep this side of me silent, and unless I get very excited, I can keep it within me. Occasionally, I speak my father's talk, and a visible amazement makes itself obvious on my caregiver, other caregivers, and the canines within earshot. When this happens, a wave of power runs through me, and I know among the canines that I am the alpha. My caregiver approves, and I feel as though he is very proud of my capabilities and is beginning to understand the whole me.

My caregivers give me many things. I have a large stash of toys and gifts which they often provide me, and access to large quantities of food. I am not accustomed to having so much, but I appreciate everything I have and often share with others.

Sharing is new to me, as to share before could have meant I would not survive, since everything necessary was either scarce or difficult to obtain. I am learning daily how grateful I can be, and when I share, I bring this gift of gratitude to other canines.

Sometimes I find it amusing to try new things in order to better understand my position in this clan. One day, my caregiver was making his meal. I already had mine in place, but the smell of his was much better. I decided to attempt a distraction, a trick which I found useful before, and see if I could obtain access to his meal, thus making it mine.

I walked into the dining area and into the space which goes outside, and I stared at the closed door. I know how to access this opening but found out early that it is not permitted, so I never perform this operation. For those canines reading this, simply get on your back feet, put your hand on the lever, and press down. Access to the outside is now available.

My caregiver came to the door and looked at me while listening to see if anything was on the other side. As he approached, I moved back to the other room where his food waited patiently for his return. And when he opened the door to see what was on the other side, I helped myself to one of the meal portions awaiting him and left the room.

I went out the special door to my area outside, ate the tender morsel, and listened carefully. I expected the angry words but heard only laughter. My caregiver was amused that I skillfully obtained the food without his permission, and for this, I was very proud. I knew at that instant he approved of my cunning. He did ask me not to do it again, and I just might consider his request.

A half moon ago, I had the inside pain, just like when I was alone at the place with water nearby. I get this every several moons, and always have. I knew my caregiver would know of this by my actions and behavior, so I waited until he asked me to come to him.

He would attempt to give me the bad-tasting morsel for several days, and each time he tried, I would offer resistance. This is the way it always has been, and since I get better each time we do this, I am fearful to change anything in my actions. As always, in a few days, I became better and went back to normal.

I love to hunt. It is a big part of my existence and the reason I am capable of living anywhere, either by myself or with a pack. My caregiver knows of this, and he makes it possible every day for me to hunt in the early morning when the sun is low in the sky and the temperature is cool. Often, my caregiver asks me urgently to leave something alone. Occasionally, I comply.

I believe this is why my caregiver decided to do this thing to me. He caught a large footless creature of very much interest to me and allowed this thing to grab my nose with its mouth. It didn't release, and I dragged this big thing throughout the dwelling for several moments until it finally released. To this day, I will not approach one of these footless things for fear that this bad thing will happen again. While hunting, I often see or know of these things, and I always give them lots of space. I feel this action by my caretaker was to protect me from harm, and now I respect his request to leave certain things alone.

I have my favorite things to catch and eat. The best is the wiggly end of a lizard. I find it easily disconnects when I grab one, and I can enjoy this treat many times from the same lizard, as they rapidly grow new ones. The first lizard I ate made me very sick, so I never repeat this mistake.

As it becomes warm outside, I enjoy my time outside earlier each day, which makes it more possible to find, catch, and eat rabbits. They are a close second to lizards, and because they are so fast and stealthy, I find the ability to easily capture them to be difficult for my caregivers and most of my canine friends to comprehend. This sets me aside in their eyes as someone special, and I enjoy this reverence.

My father is very good at this feat, and somehow I obtained the capability, though I never hunted with him. I know he is good at catching rabbits because I find his scent over many of the rabbit parts remaining in this area, even though he shares his meal with others. I will never forget his scent, and finding it on occasion comforts me because it means the Others have not broken up his pack.

I am teaching my pack, which on occasion consists of two German shepherds, two Rhodesian ridgebacks, and a rascal named Vincent, whose derivation is somewhat wild as is mine. Various groups of us hike several days a week, with me being the only one of us who gets to go every day. As we progress through the area I know and love, I show each of them where to look for rabbits, chipmunks, and squirrels. They seem able to find the lizards themselves.

I do hike with other canines that are less interested in finding game but enjoy running with me, anyway. They are all smaller, fluffy, and would normally be considered a food group by my other side; but since they accompany caregivers, I allow them consideration as canines. I teach them defensive tactics at the grassy place when their caregivers allow it, and I am amazed they pick up the important parts easily. It must be in their blood, as it is well embedded in mine.

I am very, very fast. I know this because everything I chase seems to be very slow. My caregiver knows this because the thing that makes noise was placed on my collar once, and after I chased and caught up with a jackrabbit, my caregiver looked at this thing, and there was happiness in his heart. I hear him talking of this time with many other caregivers, and he brings out this thing that makes noise, and they look at me in amazement. I know I am once again being revered, and once again, I am very pleased.

At the grassy place, there are very fast canines and some very, very fast ones. I can keep up with the ones called greyhounds for brief periods and occasionally catch up with them, but they can run like this for many moments.

My speed is reserved for overtaking food groups, not irreverent play, so I am limited in endurance; but for me and my caregiver, this limitation is not a factor. I spend much of my time in the grassy area understanding the behavior of other canines and their caregivers so I can adjust my behavior to fit in.

Today, the morning is mine, and caregivers with their canines have decided to join me and my caregiver for an early morning hike. The shepherds and ridgebacks are with us, and because of the meticulous preparation of my caregiver, we get to spend several hours in my favorite place. I am ready, my caregiver is ready, the other canines are ready, and we will find out if the other caregivers are ready empirically.

First, I need to set the ground rules. The other canines are noisy and are attempting to engage me in horseplay, so I set everyone straight with a quiet word or two, except for one shepherd. She needs a bit more from me in order to understand who is in control, so I grab her by the neck and toss her a few feet in the air. Now we are communicating. As it turns out, among all these canines, she is the best at learning the hunting ways—though each time we meet, I need to set the boundaries.

Within a few moments of our arrival, we are being tracked. It takes me a while to determine the number of followers, but I quickly determine there are two on the left of us and three on the right. Fortunately for them, they keep their distance as I teach my pack how to enjoy the indigent floral delicacies available— including mesquite beans, juniper berries, and manzanita berries. Each, in turn, tries them after me. Now they can live out here without fear of starving.

As we reach a high point, the coyotes band up and begin talking their talk. I look down and see they have banded, and I drop my head in acknowledgement of their existence. This group is neither the Others nor my father's pack, but a rather small group just passing through.

They see me and, knowing my capabilities through some measure of determination, decide wisely to head north to the watering place and leave us alone. I watch in amusement as the other caregivers round up their canines in fear of an imminent attack which will never occur, while my caregiver takes his measure from my behavior, and we continue with the hike.

As I begin again to lead the hike, every eye and ear is on me, watching for clues. Sometimes I look off in the distance, drop my tail, and stop breathing, just to see who cues on my behavior. I find it amusing when I look back and see not a single inattentive canine or caregiver.

I see a pair of large creatures in the distance and know them to be deer, and I immediately launch forward. I'm nearly alongside the trailing female when the other canines take my lead and follow up the steep incline.

I disconnect when the deer crash through a large cactus patch, just as the other canines finally reach my location, and look down at the caregivers. We have run about a half mile in about a minute, which is about ten times faster than the fastest caregiver, and within another minute, we are back among them.

During this most exceptional trek, we find two rabbits, three chipmunks, and about a dozen lizards—one of the best days I've recently experienced. The canines have become accustomed to my leadership, and one of the German shepherds has shown her willingness to be a front runner, so I allow her to lead occasionally. She seems to have a knack for this high level of activity, and it is a pleasure to work with her.

As we approach the transport mechanism called a jeep, I find an interesting cache. It was left by my father in a place he knows I will pass. There is a nice deer clavicle with some meat on it and several smaller pieces for my enjoyment. I have company, however, and canines come without manners, so I find the need to help them understand who is in control.

I need to repeat this several times for the larger ridgebacks who just don't get the big picture, and finally, my caregiver puts the treasure out of all of our reaches so there will be no conflict. I have shown the canines my dark side, and once they see this of me, they will never be the same again. Needless to say, within this group, there will never be a serious conflict involving me.

It cannot be said that I am the bully of the grassy area, but it can be said that I am the enforcer. I often help canines resolve their differences when I see escalation which might cause harm to one or more canines. When I approach the canines, if they see me, they will dispense with hostilities.

If they don't see me, I get in the middle of the conflict and break up the activity. The caregivers seem happy with this behavior, so I will continue as long as it is acceptable to them.

This is who I am and who I will always be—both to caregivers and canines alike.

I find my concern and cautiousness beginning to fade as my caregiver, who is called Mike, takes liberties with me which I would normally reward with punishment in some form. He handles my feet, brushes me, and gives me baths on occasion, and I seldom reward him with gratitude in any form.

I am beginning to see he is doing this out of love and concern, so I allow these things in small amounts, but never with any other caregiver present so this behavior doesn't propagate within the caregivers. He has taken me twice to a place that removes some of my coat, and I grudgingly allow this because, afterward, I am much more able to work without fear of overheating, and I am much more comfortable while sleeping.

As time passes, I am gradually more willing to tolerate more of this behavior. Life with this caregiver is becoming very pleasurable, and my attitude toward his actions is steadily turning into reciprocal love.

Sam With Hiking Buddies

CHAPTER 10

Sam's defense mechanisms are varied and extremely effective. He was born with characteristics of both breeds, and because of this, he is the greater of the sum of both parts. This fact has saved him many times and amazed both canines and humans alike. His capabilities are detected more readily by the canine population.

One day recently, several canines at the dog park were having a discussion about Sam.

Chuckie, a rambunctious pit bull mix, was talking with Barkley, Sam's neighbor. Others looked on with interest as the two talked about the resident enforcer of the dog park.

"So what makes him so special? Everyone is giving him a wide berth, except of course for the little ones. They fuss around him like nobody's business. Maybe I'll go over and rattle his cage."

"I suggest you reconsider," was all Barkley said. "You'll get an unpleasant surprise if you do," he added later.

"Well, I'm bigger and meaner, and I want that spot on the hill, so I'm going for it!" Chuckie offered as he trotted in the direction of Sam.

"Big mistake," Barkley muttered, remembering his first meeting with Sam.

It was just like a prison yard first meeting. The little ones, who play near Sam for protection, moved away. Sam pretended not to see Chuckie, who increased his speed from a trot to a full run.

Chuckie was nearly to Sam when Sam seemed to float in the air and move swiftly out of Chuckie's way, grabbing him by the neck as Chuckie slid past on his haunches. It was like someone was holding him by a tether. Chuckie slid for a few feet, winding up on his back, with Sam standing over him, still holding on.

"Guess who's my new bitch?" Sam quietly told Chuckie in a voice that seemed to come from the earth. "Are we crystal clear on this point, or do I need to provide further clarification?" Sam added while trying to make eye contact with Chuckie.

Chuckie refused to make eye contact. He knew Sam might take that as an insult, and Chuckie wanted to live and play another day. He learned respect for Sam on this day—and also for Barkley, who tried to dissuade him from confronting Sam. As time passed, Chuckie became friends with both Barkley and Sam.

How Sam Knew

While Barkley and Chuckie were talking some distance away from Sam, Sam was carefully listening to the conversation. His hearing came from his father, who could distinguish a rabbit coughing more than a mile away. The fine hairs throughout his large ears provided him range and direction well beyond the capabilities of canines.

As Chuckie approached, Sam followed his movement through ground tremors and the behavior of the small ones nearby. As Chuckie started to run, thus reducing his capability to react to changes in Sam's position, Sam moved just enough to skirt the attack and grabbed Chuckie by his sensitive neck skin, clotheslining him to the ground. The attack was over before it began.

Sam has his father's swiftness and agility, as well as a level of perception available only from a father with survival skills and hunting expertise. In addition, he was given the capability to understand canine behavior and group mentality from his mother. He also got from her his larger size, huge webbed feet, and strength. This package makes him a force to be feared and respected by both sides of his bloodline.

From both sides, he inherited strength (Mom) and a high level of mobility (Dad). His legs are lean, but very strong. His rear half is very lean, except for the huge rear-leg muscles. His chest is large and strong, allowing him to come into contact with an adversary without being injured.

Though he looks very much like a coyote, he is nearly twice as heavy and extremely fast during brief pursuits. He can keep up with greyhounds for short periods. Finally, and most significant: he can jump a six-foot wall without touching it.

"Told you so," Barkley reminded Chuckie when Sam finally let him rise and rejoin the larger canines at play. Sam resumed his watchful eye on the dog-park denizens while monitoring some coyote activity a mile or so away.

On another sunny Sedona morning, Sam and I were hiking in the backwoods behind our home. We were approached by another hiker who seemed nervous. Sam approached him and pointed to his right front pocket and didn't move.

"What's he want?" the nervous hiker questioned me.

"He knows you're packing and is waiting to see what you do next," I replied.

I decided to have fun with this nervous fellow, so I added, "If he thinks you're a threat, he'll grab your hand and tear it off your arm, just to keep you from shooting at him. He's part coyote and is used to being shot at. In fact, when he was first found in these woods, he had a nice selection of hands in his den—four right ones and, I think, a left one too. As long as he can see your hands, you should be OK."

The young fellow quickly pulled his hand from his pocket and disappeared toward the road below, presumably to preserve his capability to wipe his backside, which no doubt would be a priority once he removed his soiled underwear.

Sam's Toolkit, My View

I can only speak from observation. This is how I see Sam's combined assets and how they affect his daily capabilities.

We usually visit the dog park in the afternoon a while after Sam has completed two 5–7 mile hikes in the neighboring wooded areas. Sam enters the dog park and is greeted by the pups who know him, and he takes his place on a small mound near the west side of the park, facing all the activity.

He has a couple of games he plays with select fast pups. One is "let's get Sam," where he plays dumb and allows energetic pups to attack him while he feigns defense. He normally rolls on his back and allows the smaller dogs to try various approach methods of attack. I feel this is his way of gathering knowledge on how dogs attack their victims. Sam typically tires of this in a short time and gently shoos them off.

After a while of watching the activity, Sam will track the pups until a chase scenario comes about, where a fast dog leads a chase throughout the park. Sam will take a stalking stance and then launch into the chase, rapidly overtaking who is first in line. He never takes the leader down, but he will tag him a few times in the tail to let the leader know who is fastest.

His favorite game by far is to sit on his little hill and dare the newcomers to remove him from this prized position of honor. He has never lost this distinctive position to any one or group of dog-park denizens. The story of Chuckie is but one of many examples.

Away From the Things of Man

In the field, things are completely different. Sam is in his world here, and house rules don't apply. I think he can hear grass grow, as his acute hearing tops the list of attributes.

The first thing I noticed is he can determine how and where the origin point of any noise is located. If a coyote howls, he points to the location, and if it is within a mile, he tracks the offender's location as we hike. He shows this by randomly stopping and pointing to the coyote's new position.

If he feels we are being tracked, he moves to a high point for a few moments and listens. I always stop moving so he can hear the rascal better, though it might be unnecessary. If we are tracked for more than a mile or so, Sam will break rank and chase off the intruder.

Sam knows the sounds made by every bird, chipmunk, and rabbit as well as those of squirrels, humans, and horses walking. He can differentiate between horses, deer, and elk. He can hear a caterpillar eating twenty yards away, but he seems to have trouble hearing me call him from ten feet away. I guess he has selective hearing.

During conflicts with one or more coyotes, Sam's defense mechanisms really shine. When confronted by several coyotes, Sam determines who is the alpha male and then makes direct eye contact with him, letting him know he recognizes the leader. Clearly, this cognitive skill comes from his dad.

Before the coyotes can move into attack position, Sam races into the pack and takes down the pack leader. As he does this, the pack normally disburses, fearing the worst for their chief. A coyote's mantra is "live to fight another day when the odds are better." An injured coyote cannot provide for his own defense or bring food to the table.

Sam is nearly twice the size and weight of the largest coyotes. This, coupled with his blazing speed, make him a notable adversary, even when the coyotes number up to six. Often, a subordinate coyote pup will try to block Sam's attack on the boss, but Sam is quick to knock him over in order to get to the leader.

One time, Sam was attacked from the rear by a quick pack sibling. The youngster only got a small handful of hair from Sam's hindquarters as a reward. Sam has a hairy patch of defensive armoring I call pantaloons.

He has hair growing down his hindquarters that obscures his flank so, during an attack, the coyotes can't grab his hindquarters and hobble him. This is one of their ways to bring down aggressors or prey. If they can't define their target, they wind up with a mouthful of hair rapidly followed by a discussion with Sam.

Sam also has booties: hair that grows from above his uppermost claws and nearly completely covers his upper foot. This looks exactly like he has booties, but the effect in the field is similar to the protection allowed by boots on a human. Not only do they keep stickers from getting to the soft stuff, but they keep him from being chewed up by attackers, including biting insects.

Sam's tail is larger than any dog's I've seen. It normally shows which mode he is in—coyote or dog. When it curls up and makes a curlicue at the end, he is in dog mode. When it drops down and angles slightly downward, like a coyote's tail, he is in coyote mode.

Sam's tail is primarily used as a rudder when he runs very fast. He wags it in a circle to add stability to his hindquarters when making quick turns and drops it when he jumps to allow him greater height during a leap. Watch the movies on the website, and you can see this in action.

At home, Sam's intuition is amazing. He can tell from another room if my computer is pissing me off, and he will enter the room

I'm in and force himself between me and the offending hardware. I have used this action many times to explain my delay in completing this book.

Sam's Booties, Pantaloons, and His Big Webbed Feet

During the evening while we sleep, Sam monitors activity outside. He knows where all the coyotes are hanging out, lets me know if the javelina are sneaking around in the yard looking for the birdseed I keep hiding from them, and on one occasion, he kept a deer from eating one of my new trees to the ground. He doesn't bark at these events, but he makes his presence known more discreetly by gently nudging me so at least one of us can sleep without interruption.

Sam has learned to bark from his dog-park friends. He barks occasionally at the park, but he only barks at home if I am screwing with him by hiding his food or trying to sneak up on him. If someone sneaks in, they will have a heart attack when they see a pair of yellow eyes approach them from deep in the hallway, but he will not bark at them. He will give them one chance to exit the building. If they don't leave, their family won't recognize them at their funerals.

Note: He might tear off their hand if he thinks they are armed with a gun, however, whether or not they try to leave . . .

Father, Mother, and Sam

Father Painting

Sam's Mother

Sam Painting

Sam Teaching Vincent

CHAPTER 11

I had to leave town for a week shortly after acquiring Sam and was very fearful he would take this behavior as an affront to his lifestyle. Linda decided to take him to one of our favorite hiking spots for a morning excursion in which she hoped to bond with him. Fortunately, things went well. Here's how Linda described the experience.

Sam's First Walk with Mommy

I was scared to death I might do something wrong and Sam would run away. We didn't have time to create that unbreakable bond we so wanted beforehand. I loaded Sam up in the jeep, and we were off.

I took him to a part of the forest that was teeming with rabbits and very fast lizards. There were lots of smells and bushes to mark. Things were going well. I had him on a long leash, and he was doing his best to drag me every step of the way.

His strength was a definite challenge for me. I was switching from hand to hand and was about ready to give up when a friend of ours and his two collies showed up. Sam saw the collies and almost dislocated my shoulder as he dragged me (literally) for about twenty feet.

The oldest collie's name is Pal. His sister's name is Brook Lynn. During all the meeting and greeting, my friend Rick took the leash and helped dust me off. Since Sam and Brook had taken a shine to each other, we all began to walk together.

Rick still had control of the leash and found it was more work than he thought. Much to my chagrin, Rick reached down and let Sam loose. I screamed, "NO! We will never get him back. Mike will kill me."

At about that same moment, Brook spotted a rabbit, and the chase was on. Sam took off like a bullet with Brook. Oh well, I tried. Rick kept saying, "He'll come back." After about ten of the longest minutes of my life, here came both Brook and Sam looking tired and proud.

"What's that in his mouth?"

It was the cottontail they went after. Sam put his foot on it and peeled off the skin, then he offered it to Brook who looked at it like YUCK! Sam had chosen a pack partner. Rick and I just stood there in shock. Sam had taken care of himself for the first year of his life, and this was a grand gesture on his part.

The first outing turned out to be a success. I don't know if it would have turned out differently had Rick and his collies not joined us. I try not to think about it. Sam and I owed them a big favor—one that Sam would repay by saving Pal's life some time later.

Get Along, Little Dawgy

Occasionally, when the grass is high and the weather is cool, the local cattle ranchers move their herd through our hiking area. When the rains have been good, there is plenty of grass and water.

There is a man-made tank some miles up in the hills normally used by the local wildlife, deer, elk, coyote, and a myriad of other locals, and that is the primary watering source for the cattle as well.

We had buried our precious Sarah under a rocky knoll where she could watch the days come and go, be warmed by the sun, and be watched over by the stars at night. She had been there in her earlier days to see the cattle flood through the valley; most of the time, it was mothers and their new calves. Sam had yet to experience this event.

It was a normal Thursday morning walk. The three of us planned a long walk with a picnic on a large rock ledge with a view of the valley below and the red rock formations at our backs, followed by a gentle nap for all with our tummies full, the fragrant breeze inviting us to doze.

We heard the drovers first with their whistles and commands, then the unmistakable moos and the sound of thundering hooves. Sam was on his feet, ears straight up, alert and a little confused.

We were safe on our perch, but Sam was not buying it. We had also parked the jeep high on the hill out of the range of the new arrivals. We knew that the one thing the cowhands did not need was Sam in the way. In addition, the last thing we needed was Sam in harm's way. This was a mixed herd and smaller than most, but there were bulls mixed in with the cows. Lots of bulls . . . big bulls!

We decided that today was not the day to introduce Sam to the new occupants of the area. We had to leash Sam, and with some coaxing, he got into the jeep, and we were all safe for the day.

We also knew that once the salt licks had been placed and the herd spread out and got comfortable, there would be plenty of room for all of us.

We knew many of the herders from years past, and they waved as they passed us and the jeep. They were accompanied by their two cattle dogs that I'm pretty sure Sam wanted to meet. I envisioned the things they could tell him about what it was like to travel with real cowboys and horses and steers and hard work and nothing but dust in the eyes for miles. Boy, what a great job that must be, he would have thought.

After a long and enjoyable weekend of walks in other areas and trips to the dog park to see and play with all his friends, it was time to take Sam back to the old hiking spot and see what he actually did with the strange new occupants.

We parked up on the ridge so he could get a look at the cows below in the valley. He stood at the edge and became completely still. Then, like he had been shot from a cannon, he slid down the cliff and cut through the group. He was running and bouncing and barking.

Barking? Sam never barks. He was trying to get them to play with him. We laughed hysterically at the complete lack of interest from the cows. Somewhat disappointed, Sam made his way back up the cliff and stood bemused, his tongue hanging almost to the ground, ears flat, and tail wagging. He looked at us as if to say "they're no fun, they won't even chase me."

We all began to walk together, with Sam running off to chase a rabbit or a lizard. Then he spotted another cow—only this one was bigger. Surely, this one would play. This one was up on the high ground, so he must be better than the sluggish ones down in the valley. Sam set off to visit his new friend.

Sam rushed across the brush, tail in the up position, which means play. Suddenly about six feet from the new cow, Sam skidded to a complete stop. This cow was much bigger than the other ones, darker and with a different set of accessories. Sam stood still.

The bull lowered his head and snorted, then kicked dirt with his front hoof. Sam made a brilliant decision in this case; flight is the better part of valor. We continued our hike and realized Sam had gone off and had not returned. We heard him barking and some sounds of protest from the female bunch of the group.

We went to where we could see the activity, and the laughter began again. Sam was breaking the group into smaller groups and herding them into smaller groups. We were impressed by his technique. He actually looked like he knew what he was doing. If someone tried to get out of line, he would quickly restore order.

It was getting late and we had been out for a couple of hours; time to go home for dinner. We called Sam, and reluctantly, he joined us at the jeep. He was dragging, and I have never seen him so tired. He would sleep well and dream of being a cattle dog. Little did he know that, not much later, he would find two of the missing cattle that had been hiding after the herd was moved.

A few weeks passed.

The cowboys were out on horseback one day where we were hiking and asked if we had seen a pair of missing cows. We said no, but maybe Sam had seen them during his travels to and fro. Their cattle dogs had been all over the grasslands below and failed . . . you know what's coming.

Sam kept looking at the cliffs and steep wall of volcanic rock above us. Once we focused, we all saw movement up there. Mike sent Sam up the rugged rock-filled steep slope, and he herded the pair down the west side and back to the grasslands, and then he came back to us and the cowboys. It goes without saying that we let the cowboys go with Sam.

The cowboys talked to him and gave him a great deal of praise. Their dogs spent a few minutes with Sam, and the three of them played and drank lots of water. When they returned to where we were waiting, they had the two missing cows, and Sam was trotting alongside the horses, smiling. They thanked us for the use of Sam and said that he could work with them anytime.

Sam: coyote, retriever, cattle dog.

Saving Pal

It was late in the day when Rick called, frantically begging for Mike's help. Rick and the collies, Brook and Pal, had been hiking in our favorite spot. When Rick was ready to leave, he could not find Pal.

Pal is old and crippled with arthritis and bad hips. Rick had been looking most of the morning for him—calling him, honking the horn, all the things Pal knew as signals to come.

I had been to the store earlier in the day and saw a flyer for a lost sheltie. It looked just like Pal, except smaller, of course. The description matched Pal in coloring and age. He had been lost in a park about six or seven miles from the hiking destination. There was a $500 reward for his return.

When I told this to Rick, he immediately suspected that another car parked close to his had seen Pal without Rick and assumed he was the lost dog and kidnapped him. Pal was sweet and would go with anybody who was kind to him.

Rick started posting inquiries on the Internet and at the shelter, calling friends in the area to help. This saga began around noon, and it was now getting dark. Pal would probably not make it through the night if he was still there. He was old, and the coyotes would find him easy prey.

Mike suggested he take Sam out and have Sam track him. After about a half an hour of frantic searching, Sam called to Mike. He raced in the jeep to the location, and there was a very tired, thirsty, and frightened Pal.

Mike and Rick loaded Pal into our jeep and took him to Rick's car. Rick had parked in the usual place, hoping that if Pal was out there, he might crawl into the car and wait.

Here is what we think happened. Someone in the parking area saw Pal, thinking he was the lost dog and, probably driven by the reward, took him and made the call. When they found out that it was the wrong collie, they returned him to the hiking area where they found him.

Of course, by then, many hours had passed. Rick and his wife had been heartsick at the thought that they had lost their Pal. They had adopted him from collie rescue when he was just a puppy.

Rick took his Pal home. I imagine to the waiting arms of Diane, Rick's wife, and a worried Brook.

Another rescue, a favor returned.

Pal is home now and far less inclined to wander off. In addition, both Rick and Brook are very watchful of Pal's presence during hikes. The saga has strengthened Brook and Pal's friendship, and Sam is very proud to have been involved in saving Pal.

Sam Saving Pal

CHAPTER 12

Sam Saving People

Linda's Most Non-Triumphant Hike

There was a soft ticking sound on the skylights during the night. We woke to the sun gleaming like a sea of diamonds on a fresh coating of snow, so quiet and bright. Sam says, "Let's go for a hike!" He was jumping and whimpering like someone who had been kept inside too long, so we give in to the request and all don our cold-weather clothes. Since Sam's feet are too big for his body and covered in fur, looking a little like snowshoes, he went as is.

I should have known the day would come and my years of hiking luck would finally run out. I needed a miracle that day, and Sam was there to deliver it.

We were walking and crunching on fresh snow, giggling like kids, Sam running in circles yipping along with us. Then we decided to go behind one of the red rock mountains so typical of Sedona. We have made this climb a dozen times. By now, the snow was starting to melt, and the ground was becoming unsteady.

We were about two-thirds around the mountain when I reached out to step on a ledge that Mike and Sam had already traversed. The ground gave way and I fell, feet first, down the mountain, bouncing on my back until I hit the bottom. I landed straight legged on my left foot. For the first time in my life, I broke a bone, judging by the loud snap I heard! Mike called down and asked if I had broken my walking stick. Sadly, the answer was no.

In a manner, I did—my left-leg walking stick, to be exact. I was cold and a little worried as I checked my neck, arms, hands, and fingers. I lifted my left leg, and my foot dangled free. This was not good.

Mike tried to help me up, but the pain and my inability to walk at all with one leg made it impossible. I tried to put my foot down and heard another snap. "Ouch!" He managed to drag me across the wash to a bank where I was to lie in wait for what seemed like an eternity to be rescued. Sam quickly washed my face with warm welcome kisses.

Mike had to hike out quite a distance until he could get a signal with his cell phone. Sam stayed with me. We worried together. I was grateful not to be alone. We were lying in melting snow, and I was wet to the skin. That little blessing probably kept me from going into shock.

Mike returned telling me that he had called the rescue teams, and they were on their way. He said he needed Sam to help. Off they went. It was an hour and a half before I saw the face of the first paramedic and Sam.

What had transpired on the other side of the mountain was the miracle. The first ambulance arrived and got stuck. The second ambulance, an all-wheel-drive six-wheeler, made it closer, about a mile and a half, breaking a bumper but persisting with the first team of four.

Mike and Sam had been making trips to the main road about six miles out and leading the teams as close as they could get. Then it was up to Sam. Mike left him with the first team to help them find their way to me. Sam arrived first and started kissing my whole face. The paramedics were amazed that Sam would patiently guide them and their equipment so accurately, let alone so quickly.

Sam left again because he knew he was working. This was not about playing; this time he was responsible for being a rescue team member.

I heard a voice a few minutes later from far away saying "Where are you?" from one of the paramedics as he spoke into his handset, and one of the members attending to me replied, "Just follow the dog."

The whole rescue took about a couple of hours and included the arrival of more men and equipment, a big wheeled cart, and a modified Polaris ATV with a gurney adapter to haul me out of the rough territory and to the waiting ambulance. All this time, Sam was in control of the movements and coordination of men and equipment.

Mike stared in wonder as Sam went through his paces. It was just like he had been trained to do this.

After we got home from surgery to repair the triple break, the only nights I actually slept through the evening were when Sam slept on the bed with me. We even said our prayers together.

The fire department gave him a little training, and now Sam is an official Search and Rescue dog. From then on, Sam wanted breakfast in bed. He got it.

After about a week, when I could finally get out of bed, Sam and Mike took me back to our beautiful red rock bluffs. I was content at home with the constant care Sam gave me, but I was going stir-crazy in the house.

They drove me to a lovely mesa overlooking the desert valley. Mike set up my wheelchair (with Sam's help, of course), and I was left there with a thermos of wine and a novel to watch the sunset. They, of course, were off on a hike.

I sat there with the warm evening breeze on my face and thanked the Lord for my guys: Sam, for saving me from my fall, and Mike, for saving my life some twenty-two years earlier.

I giggled, thinking I was not unlike a cat with nine lives. Oh, I landed on my feet okay, but boy, what a fall!

I never opened the book that day. Just watching the beauty of nature, knowing that I was on the mend and would be walking in the mornings with Sam again, and the warmth of the setting sun and probably the wine made me content and grateful. Life is good.

Sam's next human rescue was a little eight-year-old who had strayed from a camping area. Sam knew exactly what was needed of him, and it wasn't long before Sam and his charge came trotting out of the bushes, both smiling.

There have been several more rescues since: lost dogs, people, even a very special backpack.

Wow! What a dog.

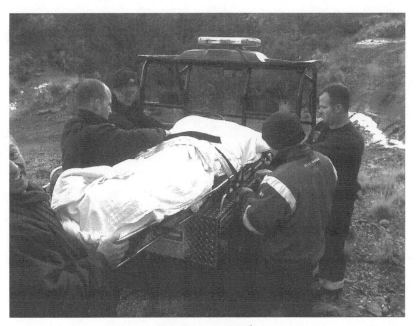

Sam Rescues Linda

CHAPTER 13

The First Road Trip with Sam

When Sam was still a puppy, we took a vacation to Taos, New Mexico. We stayed in a bed-and-breakfast made of old adobe buildings surrounding a huge grassy courtyard. Pots of fragrant flowers hung from the covered porches, attracting hummingbirds by the dozen. We sat in the old rockers made of weathered bent wood fitted with large comfortable cushions. It was so peaceful, so serene.

The spell of the quiet morning was shattered by the scream of one of the owner's prized roosters. Where is Sam? Oh no!

The race was on. Sam had the rooster in his mouth (thinking "breakfast," I'm sure), and Mike was chasing him. It looked hilarious, and I had to stifle a laugh. Around and around the courtyard they went, like a hideous carousel, Sam thinking it was a game, and Mike thinking how much does a good rooster go for?

Mike finally caught up with him by cutting him off at the giant tree that stood at one end of the racetrack. He got Sam to release the bird, which was no longer moving. Sam's mouth was full of red feathers, AND HE WAS GRINNING. Mike had a nice talk with him and began to try to scatter the feathers so no one would know.

JOKE! It looked worse, just like there had been a massacre in the farmyard.

By the afternoon, the old guy had regained his composure, sitting on the fence with the rest of the chickens—only he was partially naked. We couldn't contain ourselves. We laughed so hard, we would have to stop to catch our breath only to glance once again at the row of Rhode Island Reds and lose our composure once again. There was more to come; after all, this was only our first morning.

Then came the goats. I love goats, and there were lots of them: Nubian, Alpine, and one very scruffy one that liked to kick and bite the ears of the other goats. They called him Mike Tyson. Appropriately, Mike for short. He and Sam confronted each other one afternoon when Mike came into the courtyard. The wry goat had escaped from his enclosure and was looking for trouble. Sam was asleep on the porch. We were napping inside. The weather had turned warmer on this beautiful fall day, and it made us all lazy—except for the cunning goat, of course.

There was a bleat from the goat that sounded closer than usual, and we drifted back to sleep. It was the coyote howl that brought us to our feet. Sam!

As we emerged, they were head to head, both with their tails and heads down. Sam the coydog was in coyote mode. We called to him in a calm voice and then again, sounding firm. He could not hear us. He was about to get busy. We will be thrown out of here for sure now. We all waited in silence, including a small crowd of guests who stood frozen in time. We were waiting, just waiting, holding our breaths. Any second now . . .

It started slowly. Both the goat and Sam stood up. Sam towered over Tyson, and we thought we were in for the fight of a lifetime: the great Tyson against our coyote dog Sam.

A twitch from the goat, and they were off. Sam was chasing the goat in the oh-so-familiar racetrack, and then before we knew it, they changed places, and Tyson was chasing Sam. Sam was chasing the goat, and then the goat was chasing Sam. They were playing! Sighs of relief and chuckles filled the courtyard. All was well.

Sam in Taos

CHAPTER 14

The Pink Backpack

Often, when people come to Sedona to visit, they overschedule their time and cameras are left behind, cell phones, items of clothing shed as the temperature rises, and on one occasion, a pink backpack.

We are familiar with the West Fork hiking area and decided to take Sam for what turned out to be a chilly December walk.

During this time of year, the skies are almost cobalt blue and with a dusting of snow on the tops of the red rocks, every time you open your eyes, it looks like a postcard. We headed up to West Fork well insulated. Dry socks for us and a warm blanket for Sam waited for us upon arrival back at the jeep. Since we know about hiking in the area, we dress in layers. The midday sun is warm, and the temperatures can be quite comfortable.

We set off on our hike about 10:00 in the morning. It was about an hour into the hike when Sam, now adept at herding, kept circling Mike and then running ahead. When Mike didn't immediately follow, Sam came back and repeated the herding signal. Finally, we decided to follow. It came to a point when I had to stop and wait. The terrain was just too rocky and slippery for me; I couldn't chance another fall.

Mike and Sam returned minutes later, Sam carrying a small pink backpack. It was cute and had a picture of a kitty on the front with a bow in her hair.

I was to find out later that the "Hello Kitty" craze began in Japan in the mid 1970s. A white bobcat named Kitty White is a household name grossing about five billion dollars a year worldwide.

She appears on everything from socks and coin purses to 18k and diamond jewelry. One very special little kitty, I would say. Especially in this case, since this little bag was carrying something very special indeed, unbeknownst to us. We were about finished and cold, so we headed back to the warmth of the jeep.

We gave the backpack a quick inventory and found all the means of identifying the owners were in Japanese. Mike's knowledge of the Japanese language was pretty much limited to the spoken word, so his ability to translate what was before us was not much help. We went on home and changed into warm, dry clothes.

We went to the Red Rock Café in the village for a hot lunch, and I once again looked in the pack before we turned it in to the ranger station. There it was, as plain as day—a ticket for a jeep ride with a local tour company with the day and date clearly printed on it. At least, we could find out who they were and where they were staying. The tour was today, about an hour from now. We ate our soup and headed uptown with Sam in tow.

We arrived at exactly the same time the pink backpack owners were checking in. The next part happened so fast, I hope I can remember all of it.

We greeted the couple in their language and, poorly I am sure, told them we had something that belonged to them. Mike opened the back of the jeep, and Sam jumped down carrying the pink "Hello Kitty" backpack. He walked over and handed it to the young man. That is when everything went crazy!

There was bowing and speaking rapid Japanese and more bowing and tears, lots of tears. The young girl had, by this time, dropped to her knees, moaning and crying.

I was happy that they were happy, but all this for a lost backpack?

Another Japanese tourist was standing close and, evidently enjoying the elation, volunteered to translate for us.

The grateful pair's names were Toshi and Atsuko, and they lived near Tokyo, Japan, each with their own parents. They had known each other since they were children. They were best friends all through school, and both worked in the city. Toshi had been saving his money carefully so he could ask Atsuko to marry him and also afford an apartment for the pair in Tokyo. These things are very expensive, especially housing in the city.

He had managed the apartment fund and planned the trip to Sedona because it is a special place to make your dreams come true. He was going to surprise Atsuko with this very good news when he proposed. Since he had no money to buy her a ring, the wish to be married seemed far away.

One day, his very kind grandmother offered her ring for him to give to his lovely Atsuko. He was planning to propose to her during their hike the day before at West Fork. Atsuko had slipped and strained her ankle, so he had quickly helped her down and took her to urgent care to have her ankle wrapped.

Toshi didn't remember exactly where they had been when Atsuko fell, and he just hoped with all his heart someone would find it and turn in the cute pink backpack. You see, he had sewn his grandmother's ring into the lining of one of the pockets.

Now the exuberance was explained. We told him how Sam

had found it tucked behind a rock and brought us to it, and how he proudly carried it to the car. Toshi and Atsuko began hugging and praising Sam in a language he had never heard, but love and emotion always translates.

The Pink Backpack

CHAPTER 15

Sam has a special way with friends, and each one of them gets the privilege of behavior matched to his or her unique persona—as interpreted by Sam, of course. Sam can resolve and identify each of his friends from a significant distance, so as they approach, he postures himself accordingly. His behavior in this regard is significant and individual. Everyone and everything gets a personal response from Sam, and because of this, he is treated unusually nice by most of them. Here are a few examples.

Ellie is a huge golden retriever about Sam's age, and she possesses the exact appearance and demeanor of Sam's mom. Ellie is in love with Sam, but because he is so quick, he can avoid her advances until she tires of the game . . . unless he is on lead.

If Sam is restrained by a tether or lead, she takes immediate advantage and bestows on Sam the full measure of her affection, leaving the somewhat smaller Sam heavily slimed and usually on his back, wondering what hit him. Sam will occasionally have a discussion with Ellie, after which she cowers and becomes attentive and compliant with his wishes for a few minutes or so.

Sam's Viewpoint:

Here she comes again, the one who resembles Mom. She is much bigger than me, and that makes her slower but nonetheless dangerous since she is so clumsy. As she approaches, I send signals to her that she should interpret as somewhat hazardous, but she knows nothing of my ways. Many canines can understand my signals in posture and behavior and quickly adapt their behavior in order to survive, but not this one. She sees only the golden side of me.

I deftly step aside as she charges forward to greet me, and she turns and then tumbles by. She rights herself and then saunters over and assumes a submissive posture while licking me until I am soaking wet. I try my best not to be mean, but I occasionally have to show my teeth and have a discussion with her in order to get her to quit. Finally, she goes over to the other canines and visits.

On the opposite side of the spectrum, Cody is at the top of the canine food chain. He is very alpha and was a res-dog for most of his early years, so he has the spunk of a New York gang member and absolutely no fear. Sam and Cody met for the first time in the school yard, which doubles as a dog park during off-school hours. This is how the first meeting went.

Cody, being aggressive to all dogs, runs toward Sam with the intent of causing a disturbance. As he approaches, Sam positions himself facing Cody, drops his head and tail, and waits. Cody comes in head-on, and at the instant of potential contact, Sam grabs Cody by the neck, rolls over, and body slams Cody to the ground with such force it could be felt underfoot by bystanders several feet away.

This all happens in an instant and seems to be quite a surprise to Cody. He lies quietly, not making eye contact with Sam who is now standing over him having a discussion with him. In a couple of seconds, Sam leaves Cody alone and resumes play with one of the watching canines.

Cody remains in this position for a minute or two and then walks back to his indifferent caregiver, who is more interested in talking with other caregivers about nothing significant and who completely missed the interchange between Sam and Cody. From this event forward, Cody, when entering the play area, carefully reviews the participants, ensuring that he knows where Sam is before entering.

Sam's Version:

It looks like there is a new sheriff in town. A bully has just entered the park and is torturing all the canines I normally oversee. As he approaches, I let him know who is in charge; however, he doesn't get the message. Instead, he decides to challenge—a mistake he will soon realize.

Cody is fast, like my father, but extremely dumb. He comes in head-on, and before he knows what happened, I grab him by the neck skin and roll over, putting him in the air above me. As he rapidly descends toward the hard ground, he comes to realize his affront was a mistake.

He hits the ground hard, making a squeaking sound. I release him just before impact and am above him as he regains his senses. Now that I have his attention, I speak softly to him, and he understands. His world has just changed. He knows he is alive because I have given him a second chance, and he will get no other from me.

The other canines and their owners seem to understand what has just happened, though the owners are much slower to understand, as is normal for most biped caregivers in my estimation. Cody remains in the supine position in which I placed him, not making eye contact as I walk around him several times.

Some of the other canines come to take a look and follow me around, each saying something to Cody they would normally keep to themselves. The caregivers seem pleased at my activity, though a bit fearful of me, and that's fine with me for the time being. I will visit each of them with my ears down and let them pet me, which bonds them to me and all will be fine.

Barkley is another dog spawned from Satan and several snarling and biting breeds of canine. He has blue-brown eyes and appears to be a cross between a summer sausage and cattle dog. He is alert, fairly fast, and enough unsure of himself that every meeting offers the opportunity for physical conflict. That is, until he first met Sam.

Barkley is always curious about other dogs, so when he first saw Sam, he ran toward him with the intent of controlling the meeting. Sam, as is his nature, allowed Barkley to overcome his anxiety, but when Barkley attempted to express superiority, he got the same treatment as Cody and wound up flat on his back looking up at Sam's huge teeth.

Like Cody, Barkley was smart enough not to press the issue, and a pecking order was borne of the meeting.

Barkley occasionally tries to test the fences, so to speak, and on occasion, Sam will allow Barkley the upper hand in play; but when play gets too rough, Sam brings the game to an immediate closure. Sam knows Barkley could really hurt him in a conflict since Barkley's heritage is spawned from canines with vicious tendencies, so he doesn't push things when Barkley is agitated or insecure.

Sam Has a Discussion with Barkley (Sam's Version):

Here's another one, a canine that has been mistreated and, like Cody, has developed some bad behaviorisms. He walks like one who expects a fight every second and pushes other canines away with rough behavior and snarling teeth. He is also curious, so it is inevitable there will be a conflict wherever Barkley goes. His caregiver grabs him by the collar, which causes Barkley to snarl at him, though he reluctantly complies with the corrective move.

I know Barkley's caregiver. He visited me many times when I first came to live here, and he understands my heritage, behavior, and demeanor. I come to him with my ears down and derive some attention as a result, both from him and Barkley.

Barkley charges in from several feet away and leaves me no choice but to greet him with my other side. I grab him by the collar and toss him a few feet in the air, though he outweighs me. He flounders in the air, like a cat without a guidance system. As he tumbles to the ground, he begins to realize his greeting might have been misplaced, and just like Cody, he brings up a nice cloud of dust when he lands on his back.

As he lies there, he is careful not to make eye contact with me, which would have been difficult anyway because my mouth is wrapped around his stubby neck. He whimpers and has his tail tucked between his legs, and at that moment, he understands the order of things and that he is not and never will be at the top of the food chain here in the park.

From time to time, Barkley needs to be reminded of this order, so from time to time, I have to remind him. We often play hard, which he likes, and when he decides to push the envelope, I have to show him how rough I can play.

Fortunately, this seldom occurs, especially since Barkley's caregiver recently ran over him with his motive device called an SUV, which my caregiver calls a minivan. Barkley wasn't badly hurt, but he was very shaken up, and it has affected his demeanor for the positive.

Now for Vincent: Vincent is young, perhaps a year old, and

very feisty and playful. He is about the same size as Sam but weighs much less. Sam has an upper body like a human bodybuilder and very slim but strong hindquarters, so he outweighs Vincent by 30 percent or more. Vincent appears to be part husky, part German shepherd, and part wolf, and because he came from the reservation or shelter, his actual past is unknown.

He enjoys making sport of Sam who often sits and reviews the dog-park visitors, looking for fights to mediate or new attendees to greet. Vincent, seeing this lack of activity, often decides to stir up Sam by walking over and grabbing Sam's neck and giving him a shake.

This, of course, starts a chase scene that encompasses the entire dog-park grounds, and it often pulls in several more excited runners who would like nothing more than to get in a quick nip or two of either Sam or Vincent.

Vincent, as Viewed by Sam:

Vincent comes into the park in the presence of a young and kind caregiver. He is young and handsome himself and resembles a lupine with canine markings. He is very young and very fast and very interested in everyone and everything here, and he goes from caregiver to caregiver for attention.

Then he sees me. I sit in my viewing place, pretending not to see him. He can't resist the lack of attention I purvey on him and must take a shot at me, and I allow him to grab me by the neck, feigning anger with him. This gets him going, and I chase him through the throng of caregivers who are enjoying the spectacle. We repeat this scenario each time we visit the dog park.

I enjoy wrestling with Vincent. He is so excited to have the attention and very appreciative of the time we have together. He also accompanies my caregiver, his caregiver, and me on long hikes and has become quite the hunter.

He has not seen the Others yet, but if he does, I'll make sure he learns how to approach them and never allow him to let his guard down in their presence. They do not play games. Their strength is in their knowledge of canine behavior, just like my strength is in understanding their coyote behavior.

One thing that distinguishes this makeshift dog park from many others is that the smaller dogs do not fall prey to the larger ones. Sam seems to take the needs of smaller canines into consideration and has suggested to the larger dogs that hurting smaller ones is not acceptable behavior for this particular dog hangout. Sam is often cheered on as he breaks up conflicts that arise, and he is viewed by other owners as their savior. Now that the dog park is becoming very popular, Sam's actions are looked upon as a gift to smaller pet owners.

Many smaller dogs like to watch carefully as Sam plays with the larger ones, and they often join in when they know for sure Sam has the other dog engaged. Cindy Lou, Jake, Wiley, Lizzie, and Duncan, several of the smaller food-group-size dogs, will engage in a chase that Sam and Vincent have started, nipping at Vincent or Sam as they run along.

When Sam and another dog are wrestling on the ground, the smaller ones sneak up and grab Vincent by the arms and legs—something that would be impossible for them under other circumstances.

Bonding is what makes this particular dog gathering place so special, desirable, and fun for all participants. Everyone, including the caregivers, enjoys the canine and human interaction, and even when the weather is marginal, nearly everyone still attends. This small yard adjoining a school is a godsend for canines and their owners alike.

The Dog-Park Gang Goes on a Hike

Sam got to know many more dogs at the dog park. It amazed and delighted us that he was even the least bit social. In a short time, he became king of the dog park. Not only did he learn to play with other dogs, but he would adapt his level of play to accommodate each playmate. He would even get down low to play with the little guys.

He would stand upright at the upper edge of the grass and survey his kingdom. If some of the dogs got too rough, he would break up the fight and have a word with the players. There were also other dogs who would be allowed to go on hikes with him.

Wes and Molly belong to our neighbors who are here six months of the year. Molly is a yellow Lab, and Wes is a black Lab. In addition to this pair, in the running are Zach and Holly, both black shepherds, and the pair consisting of Simba and Kunda, both ridgebacks. Vincent rounds out the group. Vincent is a wolf, shepherd, husky mix and, to date, Sam's favorite playmate.

Sam knew he had some hard work ahead. These dogs were trained and bred for prancing around the forest, occasionally splashing in the rainwater puddles for fun. None of them ever had to work for a living. This was all wrong from Sam's viewpoint.

The first day, they watched Sam chase a deer and several rabbits. They just stood there in awe without a clue how to do these things. After a while, they would follow the hunt but run out of steam all too soon. Many more excursions later, the group kept up, much to the delight of Sam. It was time to let them know where the little water holes were and that they were a great place to cool off after a rapid chase.

The next lesson was to teach them which berries were edible. Sam had munched on juniper and manzanita berries ever since we got him. He also had an appetite for select grasses. The other dogs weren't as excited about the new edibles. Most of them, however, agreed that the mesquite beans were quite delicious when eaten in moderation.

Sam had sustained himself well in the forest and lived off the land. He had learned how to survive and stay healthy. He was very thin when we rescued him, backbones and very visible ribs; however, he was healthy and very muscular. He was to gain almost twenty pounds and grow into his feet to become the lithe machine he is today.

Meeting His Own Kind and Defending the Pack

It was just a matter of time before the coyote packs made their presence known.

Sam had his work cut out for himself when, on a perfect spring morning, a large group of six coyotes decided to make trouble. Molly, the older yellow Lab, was enjoying just walking, sniffing her surroundings, when the pack arrived.

Only one of the coyote pack made himself known. Sam and Wes chased him down to the road, and as they passed Molly, several others dropped in behind them. Molly was by herself.

That is how it works. The coyote pack will lure one of the dogs to a convenient location so the rest of the pack can attack. Sam sensed something was wrong and sped to the coyote meeting place.

He looked over the pack and picked out the leader. He sprung forward, got up on is back feet, and lunged at the leader, knocking him down. Sam just stood over him and emitted a growl I had not heard before. Wes stood by, overseeing the situation and learning at the same time.

I, in my infinite wisdom, carried a handgun which, of course, happened to be empty of bullets. I normally carry snake shot, which has a maximum effective range of about twenty feet and makes a nice loud bang—which, in this case, would have distracted the coyotes very nicely.

Needless to say, Sam saved the day.

On another occasion, a large group of hikers and their pets watched Sam disperse a group of six coyotes who had decided to track us as we hiked in nearly the same area. We were up on a small hill, and the coyotes started calling. Sam, of course, dropped from the hill and cut through the group of puzzled coyotes like a hot knife through butter.

All this time, the dogs' caregivers were yelling and screaming and calling their dogs' names. Sam stayed engaged and ran the terrified group of potential aggressors off and over the hill.

The other caregivers decided that their dogs would never hike Turkey Creek Trail without Sam.

There were many more occasions when Sam had to protect his pack. He ran off groups of javelina and coyotes regularly. He did no harm; he just let the other members of the forest know that there were boundaries they needed to respect.

I was always afraid when Sam would take off after an elk or a bull or a pack of coyotes. I had to accept the fact that he knew what he was doing. We still stay close in case he needs help, which has yet to occur.

Snake Training

The one thing we had to do with our golden was to snake train her. It is just something you do in Arizona. Rarely a day goes by without someone seeing a rattlesnake on the myriad of trails here.

Up here in the high country, there are lots of good snakes: gopher snakes, colorful racers, and many more. There are also diamondback rattlesnakes and an occasional green Mojave.

There are lots of people who give classes about how to snake-train your dog, and they charge a lot of money. Our way has always worked, and it costs nothing.

At the beginning of the snake season, we simply catch a small gopher snake and show it to the dog. He gets close enough to sniff it, and the snake bites them on the nose. Training done!

A refresher course the following season is not a bad idea.

Sam already knew about snakes. His training must have happened when he was running wild. When we hike and he senses or sees a rattlesnake, he takes us to it so we know not to bother them. He keeps his distance, and his respect for the snake seems instinctual.

He flips large rocks for lizards and can flush out a rabbit like a pro. Knowing that a rabbit will almost always run in a circle, he calculates their pattern and cuts them off at the pass.

Over the years, many of the wildlife have gotten to know Sam and come to realize that he has an ominous presence and that his demeanor does not always mirror his intent. We keep him well fed so his need to hunt for food is gone, thus making the chase a catch-and-release event rather than a death sentence for the prey.

Today, he just wants to play. The rabbits, squirrels, and lizards live to see another day.

The Dog-Park Gang

CHAPTER 16

Everyone has doubts about their position in the pack on occasion, and Sam is no exception. On this particular occasion, he had just run off yet another pack of coyotes, all descendants of the Others. The Turkey Creek hiking trail system was becoming a very nice place for canines of all sizes and shapes now that the bullies were becoming scarce, and Sam was rapidly becoming a local hero.

Sam, however, was having second thoughts about being the tough guy. This behavior distanced him from the other canines: to be so strong and independent, since canines, due to their upbringing and historical position in the place of man, have positioned themselves as weak and dependent. Sam knew he was missing out on quite a bit of care and compassion as a result of his self-imposed positioning. Sometimes, he felt very alone.

I could see this situation developing and, whenever possible, gave Sam extra care and cuddling, which he came to appreciate over time. As he grew in size and gentile demeanor, he started receiving affection from other caregivers who saw the changes in Sam and who decided to let him into their hearts. This is how Sam came to question his leadership position.

For fear that Sam's indecision would put him in peril when repelling aggressors, I decided to do some role playing with him.

I'd play the dominant pack member on occasion, allowing him to take a recessive position, and then I'd reverse the roles.

This activity allowed Sam to develop his people skills while still retaining his dominant characteristics. Once he realized that he could be both leader and follower, he became more relaxed in his unique position as a leader and developed into a compassionate one at that.

Today at the dog park, Sam played both roles to perfection. He allowed a newcomer to play rough with him, allowing the young Lab to pull him around the park by his neck, but when an aggressive res-dog came to interrupt the play, he quickly dispatched the intruder and then returned to play with the young yellow Lab.

Caregivers at the park were quick to praise Sam for his behavior, and in this manner, they reinforced Sam's position. As I watched the interchanges, it pleased me that Sam could assess his concern and work through the quandary his unique position placed him into.

Through Sam's Eyes:

I know my role in this life. It has taken me two dozen moons or more to realize that I am unique in this world around me. I see through my eyes two different worlds: the tough aggressive world of my father's family and the quieter pensive life of the canines with whom I share company.

I am comfortable in either life, but I share both worlds, and sometimes I have difficulty understanding my true position as it fits this existence. This confusion has the capability of putting me in jeopardy, as it could lead to indecision when such luxuries will create hazardous living situations. I must take a better look at my situation and erase the confusion in order to eliminate the possibility of making an irreversible mistake.

I have just corrected a pack of the Others who were tracking me and my caregiver as we hiked with a pair of canines and their caregivers. I look to my caregiver to get his approval, and he quickly praises me in front of everyone, and they look upon me with praise as a leader in my pack.

This approval comes at a price. I cannot enjoy simple play with other canines without concern from their caregivers. They know my heritage and fear that I might revert to my dad's behavior and devour their precious companions without a bit of remorse.

As I approach the caregivers to reassure them I am not to be feared, they often are skeptical and cautious—behavior significantly different from that of my caregiver. It saddens me to be placed in this position; a mix between reverence and cautious concern is always in their eyes and actions.

I am saddened by this behavior and, on occasion, consider changing my actions to conform to other caregivers' expectations of a proper canine. If I do this, I will put myself and others who look to me as a protector in the precarious position of possibly becoming part of the food chain during our daily hikes.

Today, I am muddling through this decision when my caregiver comes to me with praise for my actions, and the caregivers who accompany us mirror his sentiments, swaying me to stick to my current behavior patterns for the time being.

More reinforcement comes as my caregiver plays with me before going to the place he calls the school. He attacks me in the lethargic way humans do and chases me through the living place. Once he catches me, he becomes submissive, allowing me to attack him.

We reverse the position of dominance several times, and it occurs to me that he is teaching me how to react with other canines in the presence of their humans, and I am happy to accept his teachings.

Later, as we approach the grassy place where other canines and their humans come for recreation I feel a turning point in my thinking has occurred. I find an inner peace which has eluded me up until now, and my confidence feels restored. Now for the test.

I approach the canines in the usual way, but when one who is known to be very aggressive tries to test my resolve, I quickly and efficiently offer him a behavioral alternative, tossing him into the air as easily as a bear tosses a human.

Before he hits the ground, I'm standing over the place he will come to rest, and as he slides up to me, I whisper the words to him, and he knows from that point on who runs the show.

All of this happens in the same time it takes a drop of rain to soak into the parched earth, and none of the humans have seen the interaction, except my pack leader, who smiles as he often does when I control a situation.

This cements in my mind that I no longer have to harbor second thoughts about my actions. I have been correct all along. I walk into the park and take my place on the mound, above all others who are there, and watch their behavior, learning from each of the canines how to act and react in their human's presence.

Occasionally, I question my place here, somewhere between canine and lupine, but then I remember this day, a day of decision and resolve. I know who I am and where I fit among the creatures and humans who inhabit this place.

I'm very much like a Native American with skills beyond the ken of most humans, trying to fit the set of rules placed upon me by occasion and culture. One thing is for certain to me. I will survive and prosper in this unique and exciting world.

Sam Scaling Castle Rock

CHAPTER 17

Everyone has stories about their beloved pets experiencing their first swim or hike in the snow. Sam is no exception.

Linda is at the doctor's, I'm off work for the day, and it is snowing in Sedona. This is a most exceptional occurrence, as snow in Sedona makes the scenery take on a mystical appearance. Reds and yellows disappear, and everything becomes a distinct shade of gray, making this mystical place even more alluring.

Most people stay home, limited in movement by the Bald Eagle tires they have been nursing for ten years; so Sam, the jeep, and I start a trek toward Flagstaff where there is about three feet of snow on the ground.

We make our own road near the airport, which is closed, and suddenly are in a forest of pines, each holding a bouquet of ice crystals and newborn snow. The birds are walking today—too cold to fly, I'm guessing. They walk faster as Sam tunnels toward them, making quite a sight as he occasionally surfaces like a whale in white water to see what's going on above.

Surprisingly, a pack of three coyotes comes by to see what is making all the noise. This turns out to be an unfortunate mistake for them, as Sam surfaces and sees them trying to sneak away. Suddenly, he becomes airborne, skipping over the snow rather than tunneling, and the trepid coyotes become victims instead of curious onlookers.

Sam chases them across several fields, catching one by the tail in the process, and once he has them about a mile away, he disengages and returns to me, triumphant though only partially visible in the mound of snow on which I stand.

I've always wondered why Sam never tries to dispatch the coyotes when he encounters them. Does he sense a kinship, even though most of them regard him as a food group? He won't tell me, and I don't want to look like an idiot by asking him, though I know from experience that the only dumb question is the one which remains unasked.

While I muddle through this thought process, Sam is busy. He has found an elk trail and is following the tramped-down snow to see if he can find something to pester. He does and, as is customary for him, runs the frightened pair directly toward me.

I'm pleased to see the elk in such good condition; the weather up here seems to do them justice, and the hunters are somewhere else, probably drinking themselves senseless and talking about the ones that got away.

The elk stop about a hundred yards from me, paused in indecision as to how to proceed. Sam also stops since his running is exclusively dependent on their actions. They lie down; he lies down, and for a moment, there is absolutely no sound.

This wondrous moment of silence is broken by a pair of kids on sleds who saw Sam from a hill above and wanted a closer look. Sam decides to go visit with them, and the elk slowly walk toward the closed highway nearby.

The kids get Sam on the sled and cautiously pull him toward a small hill just below me. I watch as Sam decides what to do next, and he willingly accedes to the kids and their task. He knows speed very well—since he has run with me while I bike on the Sedona trails, too early to encounter anything but a few animals—and leans into the turns as the sled banks between adjacent mounds of snow.

Only after the sled stops does he jump off, returning to the kids above, who now have the task of walking the several hundred yards in new snow to reacquire their precious conveyance.

I hear an anxious mom call to the kids, and they reluctantly reply. She is pretty, young, has been divorced for seven years, loves Sam, and is very talkative, so the next thirty minutes gives me significant insight on why she is still not married.

We part with a handshake (no kiss), and she bundles up the kids in some sort of jeeplike vehicle and heads north to Flagstaff, I'm assuming, where hot soup and sandwiches will chase away the chill.

Sam is off somewhere trying to climb a tree. I can hear the scratching of his claws as he ascends and finally find him about ten feet up into a branch-filled pine of some type. He is interested in a chirping noise above, and though I initially see nothing, I see snow dropping from a branch high above. Sam gets about another five feet above me before he decides he is probably not going to capture the mysterious thing.

His descent is nothing less than amusing. I hear sliding-scratching noises and look above to see him slinking down backward, all the time looking over his shoulder to measure his progress. When he is about six feet from the ground, he disengages and drops out of sight in the show. He takes one look at me and heads toward the jeep, satisfied he has experienced all there is today.

On the way back to Sedona, we realize the highway coming north is now being cleared, allowing myriads of flatlanders access to the ski slopes above Flagstaff. I'm pleased to note my access route to the area still has only one set of tracks (mine), and I proceed back home, confident I'll see no other traffic. Sam lies down in the back of the jeep, probably assessing his morning and planning on having baked chicken, cheddar cheese, and a bit of dry dog food for breakfast in bed when we return home.

Sam in Snow 1

Sam in Snow 2

CHAPTER 18

Sam's First Swim

At least, as far as we know, he had about eighteen months of outdoor life before we adopted him.

As the first summer with Sam progressed and the weather began to make itself felt, Sam started looking for water. He could find water where none should be, and he found pools in which to lie and drink in the most peculiar places on the Sedona area trail system.

While he taught me the nuances of the trail system, according to Sam, I began to realize the extent of his travelling range while he was free-ranging and alone. He showed me where he used to live (a place called Buddah Beach by the VOC residents) and his den, where I grabbed a couple of his keep-things to take home. It was during this trek that I realized Sam had capabilities I never imagined.

As we approached the rapidly running stream that is a part of Oak Creek, Sam noticed some movement on the other side. He immediately began to run, and when he hit the water, he must have been going about forty miles per hour. He crossed the stream in a dash, but just before he got to the other edge, the thing he was interested in moved, and he stopped his forward progression. Immediately thereafter, he sank to his neck in water.

Fortunately, this occurred just before I stepped into the creek. The water was about four feet deep, but he made it look like it was just a few inches in depth. Sam had just run across a stream several feet deep. I'm assuming he was moving fast enough at the time he hit the water to allow him to get across. One of these days, I'll try it in the jeep to test the theory—or maybe not. It's probably best to leave that one alone.

Sam Teaches Vincent to Swim

Vincent is one of few canines that received the gift of Sam's knowledge in a variety of ways. Today, Vincent, who doesn't seem to care for water, will learn to swim. Sam has determined that this will happen, unbeknownst to Vincent.

We start the hike from a lot near the Turkey Creek trailhead and move across the road to Upper Baldwin Trail, which winds around between Cathedral Rock and the creek, giving Vincent the illusion he will never get near the water. Sam has decided on this approach since he picks the trails we will be hiking by leading us to the appropriate trail sites.

We start uphill, finding rabbits and chipmunks to entertain Sam and Vincent along the way. The two canines romp a bit as we trek uphill, and the view is spectacular. Vincent's caregiver decides to get a better look at one of the nearby outcroppings, interesting Vincent in the process. The two of them enjoy both the view and exhilaration of being at the top of the world.

Sam and I continue the trek toward the creek, enticing Vincent along. As we approach the creek, Sam smells the water and picks up the pace, which makes Vincent want to move faster. Timing is everything. As Sam slips into the water, Vincent is at the point of no return, and in order to avoid immersion, he steps on Sam's back.

Sam slips Vincent off, and lo and behold, Vincent is swimming and actually likes it. Once again, Sam exposes Vincent to something, and that something becomes a thing to like. These days, it is a rare week indeed if Sam and Vincent do not get together for a long hike, swim, or both.

Vincent and Caregiver

Sam Teaching Vincent to Swim

CHAPTER 19

Eventually, everyone has a bad day. Here are several examples. In each case, Sam was able to give every one of us some advance notice of our condition, allowing us the opportunity to minimize each event's impact. Unfortunately, we are human and very slow learners in the animal kingdom. Sam has intuitive insight on both human and canine physical and emotional conditions, and on occasion, he feels the need to let us know. And for this we are thankful, when we listen.

The Tooth, the Ear, and the Shoulder

The day started with a visit from my daughter, who tries to keep up with me occasionally on cycling excursions through the national forest area surrounding Sedona. This makes for quite a bit of enjoyment on my part, and education as well. The words that come out of that girl would make a soldier blush, and my vocabulary is constantly enhanced as we trek through trails strategically placed between cactus, rocks, and steep cliffs.

As we round a tight turn in the trail, or should I say as I round the turn, Lisa takes out a couple of branches from a low-hanging juniper and exhibits her prowess at unique vocabulary. I meander down the trail a bit farther, and Sam joins us for the remainder of the ride.

Sam knows how to run with bikes, horses, deer, elk, and other slow-moving creatures. Given his capability to run very fast, he lopes along either in front or just behind the pack, unless something of interest comes by and captures his attention. After he deals with the object of interest, he'll race up behind us and resume his position.

We travel for a couple of hours, winding up the ride at the same place we started. I load the bikes, dog, and Lisa into the jeep, and while I am doing so, Sam takes an interest in Lisa that is not customary.

Lisa is sitting in the passenger seat, and Sam reaches from the seat behind and licks Lisa's left cheek, alternating between licking and sniffing. This goes on during the trip back home and for the remainder of the evening until Lisa leaves for home.

The event fell into the forgotten pile for a few days, and then we get a call from Lisa. She had some discomfort from an old filling, and when she went in to get it reviewed by her dentist, he determined she needed to have a root canal. The tooth had been seeping poisonous fluid for several days, a condition that could have become very serious if left unattended. The tooth was one of those on her lower left side.

A couple of weeks later, when Lisa came back to Sedona for some more punishment, Sam immediately checked her left cheek. Apparently, he was satisfied that she was OK, as this occurred only once during the visit. Though Sam went with us on several hikes and one long bike ride, he didn't repeat the incident, but we are now very careful to be watchful of this type of behavior from him.

Sam's View

I enjoy visits from my caregiver's kin, especially the one called Lisa. She is a subordinate who has a very nice personality and good demeanor, quite unlike most humans in this pack. She uses the words of anger quite often, particularly when trying to keep up with me and my caretaker while using the two-wheeled things. This amuses my caregiver and pack leader each time she speaks them, so I do not fear the words when they come from her.

Something smells wrong with her. I know this from my extensive experience in caring for myself and from the many canine visitors to my first real living place, the big place called Humane Society. Many of the canine visitors who came there were in pain and needed caregiver help to get better, including me on several returning occasions. I will check this out in more detail when she is at my level of height.

Even with the two-wheeled things, humans are much slower than me, so I can enjoy my visit to the area with trees and living things in my normal manner and then quickly locate and catch up to them. I leave all things human, including the large creatures some of them sit upon, well enough alone, since introducing me as a variable often is confusing and causes fear among them.

We have a nice long visit, with many angry words and laughter about the excursion coming from the humans and also several opportunities for me to run with fast-moving native creatures. I no longer catch and eat them since I am well cared for by the humans, but I will never forget who I am, in case this living situation with which I am so happy changes for some reason.

Among the canines, I am the only one I know of who is able to enjoy two types of existence. I can be a canine who lives with humans and obeys their rules, and I can have my other side, which is capable of self-sufficiency if necessary and which has dominion over all things that roam in the wooded areas.

This life is unimaginable by the other canines and equally unimaginable by those who share the part of me which roams the woods. They must fight every day for necessary sustenance and have none of the luxuries which I currently enjoy. I saw one of them earlier today and sent him packing across the creek where, presumably, he cussed at me using the lupine version of Lisa's angry words.

As we leave the hiking place, I notice a strange thing about the human Lisa. She has something bad growing inside her mouth which, in my estimation, could possibly cause her great harm. I lick her on the side of the face where it lives inside her, trying to make her aware of this bad thing, but my concerns go unnoticed.

Several times during the remainder of her visit, I try to announce my fear for her condition. It is very bad that humans do not have the capacity to understand my sensitivity to their delicate physical issues.

The next time Lisa came here for some more education regarding the two-wheeled things, I immediately reviewed her condition and was very pleased to see that she had made the necessary changes. The bad thing was gone, and she was in much better condition, though fixing this thing did not fix her use of the angry words or improve her capability to make the two-wheeled thing go in the prescribed direction.

On another such visit, my pack leader and caretaker seemed to be in another place. He was not as attentive and cognizant of things around him in the customary manner. I could smell a bad thing inside his head, but he didn't allow me to get close enough to find out exactly where the bad thing was living.

Finally, when he rested, I carefully approached him and found the bad thing to be in his right ear. It was still too small to cause him discomfort, but it clearly was affecting his ability to perceive things by listening, and he occasionally did not understand the human Lisa's words when spoken on that side.

During an excursion with the two-wheeled things on the second day of Lisa's stay here, we were able to notice my caretaker's discomfort. It was now apparent to him there was an issue he needed to address in his ear. He attempted to resolve the issue using water and white flexible things he occasionally uses to dispense sticky medicine to me. He was unsuccessful and reacted distastefully to the attempt.

A visit to the doctor was in order, and after he returned, I noticed the thing was getting smaller. After a few days, he was all better. He thanked me in the customary way, with words and kind gestures, and I knew he was finally aware of my attempts to help him find and correct the problem.

My Take

Call me stupid, as I'm certain Sam does. He tried to let me know about the broken eardrum in his customary way, by licking my ear and nudging me while I slept, but I ignored him. I took Lisa for a nice long ride, and the entire time, I felt like certain customary noises and the occasional burst of profanity from Lisa were somewhat distorted.

As the ride progressed, I began to grow a headache in the left temple, which got progressively worse. Sam noticed everything, of course, and gave me the look he reserves for those who do not listen to his suggestions. I made the decision to go to Urgent Care as soon as Lisa started her trek down to the Phoenix area, and Sam made sure I carried out the objective.

I had one more thing to try before committing to a doctor visit. I thought I had a bit of blockage and tried to remove it using one of those magic ear wash kits, but once the fluid hit my eardrum, I nearly blacked out from the pain. Now was the time to swallow my pride and head out to West Sedona.

When I returned, Sam made me sit down so he could inspect the situation. He backed away from the medicine inside my ear and gave me a look of approval. And of course, he checked my progress daily until he was satisfied I was better. Needless to say, every time Sam shows interest in a particular area, we take a bit of extra time to thoroughly check things out; and also needless to say, we usually find something that needs attention.

Even Before You Feel the Pain

Linda walks with Sam and me on occasion, and recently we took her for a rather long one, which encompassed a large wooded area behind Cathedral Rock, one of the most photographed areas in Arizona. Sam was preoccupied with Linda, and on many occasions during the trek, he walked around her as if herding her to an as-yet-unknown destination.

When we stopped for a quick respite, he trotted over to her and put his hand on her right shoulder and nuzzled her for a bit. He finally came over to me for a drink of water and then went back to Linda and repeated the process.

We were out and about for a couple of hours, and each time we stopped, Sam gave attention to Linda's shoulder and even whined a bit when she got up using the shoulder as a pivot point against a rock outcropping against which we rested.

Later in the evening, while we were wrapping up evening activities, Sam took a place next to Linda on the couch and rested his head gently on her chest, paying more attention to the shoulder. Repeated inquiries as to the condition of her shoulder were dismissed, and we all went to bed, with Sam taking a spot between Linda and me.

Sam got the nickname "cotblocker" from one of my friends while commenting on Sam's decision to take the middle spot when the three of us went to bed, so this behavior in itself didn't register concern from either Linda or me. The behavior Sam exhibited during the day did not make itself obvious until the following morning.

Linda got up to a sharp and persistent pain in the shoulder, and upon diagnosis by our local doctor, Linda wound up with a shot of cortisone. The shoulder still makes Linda aware of it on occasion, but the shot made everything much more tolerable from the pain and mobility standpoint. Once again, Sam knew in advance that something needed attention.

Sam Again

I feel my female caregiver's pain. She has something in her shoulder that shouldn't be there, and I feel the warmth coming from the bad thing. I am trying to let her know, but she—like all humans—seems unable to understand me.

Something in humans must be broken. We canines know when something must be attended to, but for some reason, humans are complacent. This must be why they constantly go to a different human to get things fixed.

I remember my pack leader taking me to see another human to fix my bad tummy, my sore foot, and occasionally, for no other reason than to put me on a weight-measuring thing while they stick something where something should never be stuck and then poke me with a very sharp thing that feels like cactus.

I know this place very well, and I make it obvious I do not want to return as we get close each time, but we go anyway. I hope this interaction does not dull my perceptive ability and capability to take care of myself.

My pack leader's mate uses the shoulder as if nothing is wrong. She will pay for that indifference later, once she realizes something is wrong. This night, I will protect her from further injury and sleep little.

It is the morning of the next day, and the bad spot is much worse. I can feel the heat from a full human measure of a width away, and the discomfort is finally felt by the female. Today's activity will include a trip to the human called "doctor."

I still feel the heat, but it is much less now. This problem will not go away easily, but the female caregiver is reacting much less to the discomfort, so the doctor must have made things better for her. I will keep watch on her for a few days, just in case.

Sam on Back

CHAPTER 20

Sam finally meets his dad today, and the result surprises me. I've feared this day for a long time, concerned he will chose his father's lifestyle over the one we have given him.

Sam Meets Dad's Pack

It's a nice fall day, with promise of a good hike. Sam and I are out early and plan to meet up with other hikers with pets who are interested in Sam's secret hiking spots, where everyone can run free without bothering or being bothered by anyone.

As my watch's minute hand moves over to the 6 a.m. region, we wander up a small hill where we can see pretty much everyone in the valley. No one is present on the signed trails, but we see some movement across one of the shallow washes below.

I make out a small handful of coyotes and expect Sam to assess the situation and decide whether or not to disperse the group, as he normally does in this situation.

Something is different here. Sam is watching the group, but he doesn't exhibit the killer instinct he normally displays when put in this position. Instead, he watches them carefully, his tail twitching slightly to and fro. He makes a soft whine and keeps track of the group as they move up the hill in our general direction.

"Sam, what's wrong?" I ask him.

He doesn't answer me. Instead, he continues to watch the group as they move up to a small mesa about one hundred feet below us. I walk over to him and he ignores me, still watching the group. I think about tumbling a rock down the slope to the mesa below to get them moving, but when I plod over to the edge, Sam crosses in front of me and begins his descent to the mesa below.

Normally, Sam moves in total silence. His advantage is surprise when he approaches a group of coyotes this large, and he uses that advantage to disrupt a group of coyotes into breaking their attack pattern. This time, however, he is making much more noise than is typical. The group below can easily hear him, and they mass closely around the largest male as he approaches.

Sam is clearly the largest of the group, but he is acting very submissive, which concerns me significantly. I fear Sam is putting himself in jeopardy with his actions and prepare to dispense some projectiles in their general direction if things go bad.

As Sam nears the group of coyotes below, the large one meets him head-on. Sam is still walking with his head down and ears flat. The large male walks up to him and around him several times. Sam's tail is wagging slightly, and the other coyotes move up to him, each in turn sniffing him and following the big one's lead.

I come to the conclusion that Sam has finally found his original pack leader—possibly his father and half-siblings. For a moment, I fear I have just lost Sam and that he will join his pack below, never to be seen again by me, Linda, and all his new friends. My heart sinks. I reconcile myself to this possibility and decide to accept whatever happens, as long as Sam is happy.

Sam spends a few minutes more with the group and then trots back up to me. The group watches us for a few moments and then heads north toward the creek, none of them looking back. Before Sam gets back to me, the group has disappeared into the woods below.

"Thank you, Sam." It is all I can say as waves of relief come over me.

Sam's Take

We are starting early today. I like this time of the day best. Many edible creatures are running around, and I have lots of opportunity to hunt. My caretaker has been talking with others about today, so I know we will have company, but I also know the other caretakers are afraid of the dark. They never join us until much later in the morning.

We are walking in the territory of my father's pack. I smell him and my half-siblings everywhere. I have met him several times before while foraging around out of sight of my caretaker, so I know not to show fear. I am bigger and younger than him, so I have no fear of him, but my siblings are young and strong and several in number.

The first time I met him out here, I was smaller. He will be pleased at my growth, I am sure. Though I can never live his lifestyle, he knows I am capable of protecting myself. I am more than canine and more than coyote, and I can move freely between each genus.

When we first met here in his territory, he quickly approached me as if to take me down. I easily averted his attack and positioned myself between him and my siblings. Since I was a bit larger than him, he was careful not to allow me access to his flank, but to his surprise, I stood on my hind legs and easily toppled him to the ground. My siblings slowly backed away.

My canine parts include a larger chest and stronger front legs, and he was not ready for the amount of force I could generate. Once down, he was wise enough to remain there. Of course, I let him back up, and he rejoined his pack, quite taken aback by my defensive capability.

It was at that moment I realized he was familiar. We first met when I was tied up in front of another caretaker's dwelling and very much younger. He came into the yard, sniffed me up and down, and then ate the dry food the caretakers were trying to get me to eat. He then left, slinking back into the dark night from which he came. I have always sensed that he was my father, and now I know that fact for certain.

My caretaker has climbed to a familiar vantage point from which we can watch the other caretakers approach. As we watch, I hear a familiar pattern of footfalls and know my father's pack is nearby.

My caretaker is watching me with concern. He knows something is up as I scan the area below for my father. Then I see him and his pack coming up the hill.

My caretaker looks at me and says something, but I don't hear him. I make the decision to drop to the plateau below and confront my father and his group. I will not be silent this time as I approach. I want him to be aware of my presence in advance.

I'm directly in front of my father. He looks me over, and I sense his approval. He makes no move to attack but, rather, treats me as a trusted companion and an equal. I am pleased beyond verbal conveyance as the pack treats me with both compassion and respect.

I sense he knows it is me who has moved the Others away from here. News of my presence has travelled fast from voice to ear among the coyote community, and now my father and his pack can live here without fearing attack from other packs. I know we will meet again from time to time, and I am pleased I can share in this life as well as the one my caretaker has made for me.

I climb back to my caretaker above and am greeted with both relief and compassion. Together, we watch my father and his group slowly head home to the water.

The sun is now up, and together, we watch for signs of the other caretakers and their canine companions. It has already been a great day, with more fun yet to come.

Sam Watching Coyotes

CHAPTER 21

Javelina, Anyone?

A cold night and all is well. Daddy and Mommy are fast asleep with Sam in between, all with heads on our pillows, all snoring softly as a gentle wind in the pines behind the house lulls us during our peaceful sleep. Then we hear the sound we know from experience is the birdseed dish being overturned.

We awake to see Sam sitting at full alert, ears straight up, and he emits a low growl which is barely audible. This has the whole family trying to decipher the unwanted new development disturbing our sleep. The noises outside belong to javelina!

Sam is not fond of javelina. Sam likes to chase javelina.

Javelina are not nice animals. They can be found in Arizona as far south as Tucson and as far north as Flagstaff. When visitors come to Arizona, they talk about the "wild pigs" they have seen. Not quite correct. They are collared peccaries, not pigs.

Peccaries are in their own category closer to the rodent family. They are ugly, smelly, aggressive, and will attack if traveling with a pack containing little smelly, ugly peccary babies. Their heads are very large. They only have three toes and a narrow backside, along with large angry tusks below a long hoglike snout which they clank.

They commonly weigh fifty to sixty pounds, but have been known to reach ninety to a hundred pounds. This—combined with a loud screeching snort, the kicking of the front feet, and an eye-watering smell, especially when annoyed—says "get away from me".

The first time Daddy went outside to confront the largest one of a javelina pack, the smelly intruder backed him into a corner on the patio. I had been videotaping the event from an open French door, which I quickly closed, leaving my husband without escape.

I told him he was on his own; I didn't want that thing in the house. I watched as he began talking "baby talk" of all things, but it worked. The old guy backed away and left without causing any further distress. Daddy was allowed to come back into the house.

Back to the Present

Sam wanted to protect us from these unwanted guests, *or* he just wanted a good midnight chase. Daddy let Sam out, and the other dogs in the neighborhood chimed in with robust barking, wishing they could get into the action. Sam, with head down and growling his special "get off my property" growl, ran off about three of the large fifteen-member group.

Unfortunately, one of our neighbors has been feeding them, not helping keep the damaging peccaries at bay. Sam returned to chase away more until the whole group finally took the hint.

The next night, our unwanted visitors found the small trash can where we keep the birdseed and peanuts for the blue jays. We had just filled it, so it contained about forty-five pounds of seed. The can had been "hidden" in the inside corner of the patio.

When that went over, the herd of running javelina charged the corner of the house. We peered out of the sliding glass door only inches from the monsters with steaming breaths. Sam said, "Oh, let me go. Oh please, let me go."

By then, they were slamming their bodies against the house and sliders. We let Sam chase as Daddy began the undaunted task of sweeping as much of the seed off the paver-covered floor of the patio as possible.

Mommy went back to bed.

When my weary warriors returned, they were tired and came to bed trying not to bother Mommy.

What Sam doesn't know is that javelina like to chase and attack dogs, coyotes, and bobcats. Don't tell Sam.

The colored peccary, or javelina, is colored a grizzled black and gray overall with dark fur on the shoulders. The fur is very coarse. The young are reddish to yellow-brown in color.

In adults, there is a mane from head to the rump, which is most obvious when the javelina is excited. Their vocals are divided into three alerts. They travel in numbers of six to twelve, although as many as fifty are active during early morning and evening when it is cooler.

All travel together, with the exception of the old and infirm, who prefer to die in privacy so as to continue the hierarchy wherein the largest of the dominant males control the group.

Javelina tend to stay close to water sources, unlike the coyote and other residents of the desert areas. They mark their territories by rubbing the secreting glands on their rumps on trees. The javelina's territory is fiercely defended by squaring off, laying back the ears, and clacking their canines.

In a fight, they charge head-on, bite, and occasionally lock jaws. At midday, they lounge in shade and munch on berries, nuts, and cactus. It seems they have a complex digestive system, which allows them to munch on agave and prickly pears cactus.

All of the breeding is done by the dominant male. Breeding occurs during all types of weather, especially rain. Go figure. One to three young are born after a gestation period of 141–151 days.

The mother separates herself along with the newborn's older sisters, to hide in hollow logs in order to avoid being eaten by other group members.

Needless to say, we keep our distance. We make it a point to bring in all the seed by nightfall. This seems to help. Though Sam misses the challenge, we finally enjoy sleeping all night.

CHAPTER 22

The Tail of the Kaibab Squirrel

Separated by one of nature's wonders, the Albert's and the Kaibab squirrels have an interesting beginning.

The legend of the Kaibab squirrel has always been considered truth in its purest form. I remember seeing my first Kaibab squirrel when I was just a kid. My father was telling me the story of Wilber, the Albert squirrel, and Sylvia, the Kaibab squirrel, who lived in harmony as one species. Well, officially, they were both still Albert squirrels.

Enter the Grand Canyon

Wilber wound up on the on the south rim and stayed brown and unremarkable—cute but unremarkable. Sylvia wound up on the north rim where she morphed quickly into a gorgeous midnight mink color with black tufts three inches long decorating her ears like eyelashes gone Hollywood. She had a tail to die for: long, white, and feathery. A goddess had been born.

Scientist tried to debunk this theory with talk of ice age and food supply; no romance there.

Here Is the Way I Heard It

One day, it got really cold. I mean, as in ice-age cold. Wilber, Sylvia, and about three hundred of their closest friends were in the bottom of the Grand Canyon. Some of the group wanted to go up to the North Rim because they believed they would find the best food up there.

Some others wanted to go to the South Rim because they thought since it was "south" it would be warmer and, therefore, had better food. And so began the argument the intensity of which would not be repeated until the Hatfields and the McCoys.

Squeaks got louder, and fur flew. Then Sylvia said, "Enough already!" And she headed up the steep ascent to the top of the North Rim. There, she and her followers found wondrous stands of ponderosa pine trees full of pine cones with plump seeds and truffles growing on the ground around the trees which produced wonderful nesting materials that would rival the best products from *Bed Bath and Beyond*.

The Albert squirrels finally settled on the South Rim. Eventually, the pine trees started to grow there too, and all was well. Even today, the Albert squirrel looks about the same, but it was getting more and more difficult for Wilber to call his sister Sylvia.

The following is a picture of the Kaibab squirrel as you can see them today. Note the significant differences between this pretty little creature and the ones who sneak down from the trees in your immediate demographic region and steal the precious gifts you provide for the birds in your backyard.

Kaibab Squirrel

The Official Version

The Kaibab squirrel is an example of evolution occurring through *geographic isolation.* The Albert's squirrel, with its several subspecies, has a much broader distribution and is found on the South Rim of the Grand Canyon.

The difference between the North Rim's and the South Rim's Albert's squirrels has given rise to the commonly held, but incorrect, assumption that the canyon itself acted as a barrier, preventing gene flow between the two populations.

Modern Kaibab squirrels are descendants from populations of Albert's squirrels that dispersed into the Grand Canyon area following the ice age. As the climate warmed, some Albert's squirrels migrated to the high elevations of the ponderosa pines of the North Rim of the Grand Canyon.

As the climate cooled again, the ponderosa pines once again grew at lower elevations, and the other Albert's squirrels dispersed to the lower Grand Canyon area, filling in their former niches on the South Rim.

Aaaaaaa, wasn't that what I just said?

While I discussed this section with Mike, Sam perked up his ears and said, "Squirrel, where?"

He was ready to hunt, as usual.

Praying Squirrel

Kissing Squirrels

CHAPTER 23

Sam and Mommy Go for a Walk

Sam and I went for a walk this morning. I was moving a little slower, but he was at my side. It's funny how he paces himself, never losing sight of his charge. The sun was warm for a winter day, reminding me of one just so much like it earlier this summer. It too was warm that day, so Sam and I decided to take the Boynton Canyon trail.

We usually go just past the ruins on the cliff above. This particular day, we ventured farther until we came to the large meadow toward the end of the walk. It was getting hot and was about the time we stop for a drink and a rest. Sam stopped, and a small whimper escaped his trembling body. He moved a step closer and sat down, staring straight ahead, ears fully upright.

As I looked up, it seemed as if everything, including my breath, stood still. There in the grass before us stood a huge female bear and her cubs. Watching the wonder of it all suddenly made me feel like a flea on the back of Mother Nature herself.

Having felt so prominent in the city and its workings, this was an unfamiliar observation. I have been comfortable in the wilderness since I was a child, but never so much in awe as that moment.

We stood motionless until the momma and cubs, feeling no impending danger, slowly collected themselves and moved off into the woods. It took us a minute to fully embrace what we had just experienced. Sam looked up at me, and I smiled. He knew that the bear belonged, we didn't. He respected that. I respected him for it.

The remainder of the day was uneventful, yet I couldn't help remembering the dozens of times I was too busy to see things the way he does. How much have I missed?

Sam chased lizards and a jackrabbit we call "Jumbo Jack." They have become uneasy friends over the last few years. Jack waits for Sam at what we call "rabbit crossing". Once Sam has arrived, the chase is on.

Nobody gets hurt, and both have a good run. Sam occasionally catches up to Jack, and they go their own ways, exhausted and happy. Jack has had some babies over the years, but the play is reserved for Sam and his old friend Jack.

I looked down just then and saw Jack's prints in the soft red sand. I wondered where Sam had gone. Sam returned to join me later with a face full of cactus quills. Jack won this round, taking solace in a large paddle cactus plant.

We found some shade and drank water. I began the chore of pulling the painful needles from Sam's face when he pawed my hand as if to say, "Later, Mom, let's just rest." I petted him slowly and watched his eyes close.

I joined him for a short snooze—the warmth of the sun on my face, the birds having conversations I could not possibly translate. Perhaps we were all thinking the same thing. What a gorgeous place, the comfort of friends, the blessing of the day.

Sam on Alert

Chapter 24

To Be Continued

As with all stories, there is one which, when spoken or written, gives a nice close to a book, or perhaps precedes the goodnight kiss to a young listener, closing out the evening. This is that story.

Tommy, the Eight-Year-Old, and Sam

It had been a beautiful couple of weeks near Oak Creek Canyon north of Sedona. Lots of campers were here for the last holiday weekend before the kids had to go back to school and the weather changed. Fall comes in hard some years. The leaves on the sycamore trees can change almost overnight with a freeze.

It was in the morning, just after breakfast, when Tommy's older sister noticed that he had not come back from the creek. He had wanted to go down "just one more time" to see glistening liquid make its way over the rocks and surround the grasses along the edge.

There had been ducks and heron and even a beaver to see if you kept very still. It was cooler that morning, suggesting that the weather was changing, and Tommy's mom had insisted he wear a jacket. He had cool things in the pockets like gummy bears, pretty rocks, a dead lizard, and a whistle. Just little-boy stuff—except for the whistle. You see, Tommy was deaf.

Something moving upstream caught his eye and startled Tommy. It was a deer. He wanted a closer look, and that is how his adventure started. Through the low-lying bushes and grasses he ran, never quite losing sight of the doe.

Around trees and over rocks they went. He was a boy on an adventure. He was getting winded and, just about that time, fell into a "cat's claw" bush. The sharp hooked thorns tore into his jacket. He managed to get out of the jacket, but every time he tried to take it back, the fabric ripped. He knew his mom would be mad, so he decided to leave it there as a marker and head back to camp.

Tommy looked up at the dense forest of trees and back at the pooled creek, not sure which way was back. He had crossed the creek more than once, so he had no idea where he was. If he had been a little older, he might have followed the creek, but remembering that up was the way back to camp, he began his climb. At first, he pretended to be a mountain man.

He found a long stick and used it for a walking stick the way he imagined a mountain man would. He was far enough from the creek now and should have been walking into camp. There was no camp. Tommy walked through crowded brush and tall grass for what seemed to be a very long time. Alone, tired, and frightened, he lay down under a pine tree and cried himself to sleep. He was covered in scratches and had acquired a bruise or two along the way.

Back at the camp, the family had notified the Search and Rescue teams. Others in the camp helped as well. Several problems come about with too many people looking and trampling footprints and moving clues. Everyone heard the sirens and the search party calling—except Tommy.

By the time Tommy awoke, it was afternoon, and slowly his fear turned to terror. Mom and Dad had probably left and forgot about him. Being alone in the forest was worse than monsters under the bed. He started out again tentatively, eyes wide and heart pounding. The shadows in the canyon were getting longer, suggesting late afternoon, when Tommy saw Sam.

When the searchers failed to find Tommy in a couple of hours, our friend Rick suggested it was time to call Sam. It took Sam a while to find the little boy; he had traveled quite a distance, and because it was a holiday weekend, there were tracks everywhere.

One look at Sam and Tommy fell to the ground, tears streaming down his dirty, scratched, and sunburned face. Sam washed it for him. Tommy's tears turned into low giggles. Sam signaled to Tommy to follow him by tugging on his pants leg. Up the hill they went, popping out by the road—Sam with his tail wagging and Tommy with the biggest grin his mother had ever seen.

I wonder what happened to the jacket.

To Be Continued . . .

Lost Boy and Sam

ABOUT THE AUTHORS

Mike and Linda Harris are residents of Sedona, Arizona. They relocated to Sedona in 2003, leaving California for a less-structured and more healthful lifestyle in a peaceful, beautiful place.

Both are graduates of SDSU, and Mike has authored several books under his name on technical subjects, including some which remain in the classified domain. He is from a Business Development background with emphasis on contract electronics for Defense Electronics companies, who provide subassemblies utilized in threat detection and prevention onboard aircraft and aboard ships.

Linda has a Business degree, and was most recently a Director of Resident Programs at one of the largest multi-level senior care facilities in Southern California. She has been on television, and is credited for assisting in the establishment of the ethics committee under which many of the senior care facilities operate today.

Both, with the assistance of Sam, co-wrote this book.

Both Mike and Linda are active in the Sedona area, volunteering under USFS programs which are dedicated to preservation of the Sedona wildlife preserves and trail systems. These include the Adopt-a-Trail program, Mountain Bike Patrol and Friends of the Forest programs.

Sam is included in these efforts, and routinely can be seen walking in the forest with patrollers, trail management personnel and volunteer search and rescue groups.